The Digital Classroom

Based on a major research project (the InterActive Project), *The Digital Classroom* explores and illustrates how digital technologies can transform learning across the curriculum. Using a wide range of educational settings – primary, secondary, school and home – it will help practitioners to think about, plan and support effective learning in their classrooms and beyond. Showing how teachers can 'harness technology for the future', it covers important topics such as:

- personalised learning;
- using ICT to support children with special needs;
- the use of ICT in home–school links;
- designing 'digital' classrooms;
- the management of technological change in schools;
- collaborative learning using technology;
- continuing teacher professional development.

By weaving 'evidence-based practice' into each chapter, this book will provide extensive guidance, practical advice and insights into working in the 'digital classroom' for all primary and secondary school teachers. It will offer readers the chance to examine their own practice in relation to digital technologies and enable them to understand the benefits and limitations. Throughout the volume, a number of practical exercises and reflective tasks will encourage the reader to engage with the text and contextualise each chapter within their own professional practice and experience.

Professor Peter D. John is Vice-Chancellor of Thames Valley University.

Steve Wheeler is Lecturer in Information and Computer Technology in the Faculty of Education at the University of Plymouth.

Related titles

E-Schooling
Global messages from a small island
Roger Austin and John Anderson

Unlocking Teaching and Learning with ICT
Identifying and overcoming barriers
Helena Gillespie

The Digital Classroom

Harnessing technology for the
future of learning and teaching

Peter D. John and Steve Wheeler

Routledge
Taylor & Francis Group

LONDON AND NEW YORK

First published 2008
by Routledge
2 Park Square, Milton Park, Abingdon, Oxon, OX14 4RN

Simultaneously published in the USA and Canada
by Routledge
270 Madison Ave., New York, NY 10016

Routledge is an imprint of the Taylor & Francis Group, an informa business

© 2008 Peter D. John and Steve Wheeler
Note: The right of Peter D. John and Steve Wheeler to be identified as the authors
of this work has been asserted by them in accordance with the Copyright, Designs
and Patents Act 1988.

Typeset in Bembo by
Keystroke, 28 High Street, Tettenhall, Wolverhampton
Printed and bound in Great Britain by
TJ International Ltd, Padstow, Cornwall

British Library Cataloguing in Publication Data
A catalogue record for this book is available from the British Library

Library of Congress Cataloging in Publication Data
A catalog record for this book has been requested.

ISBN13: 978–1–84312–445–0
ISBN10: 1–84312–445–9

Contents

List of illustrations   vi
Acknowledgements   vii

Introduction   1

1   Policy and politicians   6

2   Teachers and technology   15

3   Personalised learning   25

4   Whole-class and collaborative learning: working and learning together with ICT   38

5   Interactive technologies   45

6   Inclusion and special needs: access for all to the digital classroom?   55

7   Assessment and evaluation using ICT   71

8   New technologies and the curriculum   80

9   Constructing the digital classroom: management of technological change in schools   93

10   Connecting the learning community: extending classroom boundaries   105

11   Continuing professional development   117

12   Harnessing the power of technology   124

Bibliography   130
Index   143

Illustrations

Figures

2.1	Issues relating to access to resources barrier	22
3.1	Dimensions of personalised learning	28
5.1	Word parts	52
5.2	Family of words	53
7.1	Assessment sheet	78
7.2	Wokingham District Council's ICT electronic assessment form	79
9.1	Diffusion of innovations model	100
9.2	Diffusion of technologies in families with school-age children (2005)	100
10.1	Rise in UK mobile-phone ownership between 2001 and 2003	112

Tables

2.1	Barriers to ICT use	21
2.2	Factors needed for successful ICT implementation	24
11.1	The positive and negative factors in the deployment of ICT	122
12.1	Contrasting technology user profiles	126

Acknowledgements

The authors would like to thank the following:

- Mark Townsend, of the Faculty of Education at the University of Plymouth, for his significant contribution to Chapter 6;
- Dan Sutch at *Futurelab*;
- The InterActive Education Project team at the University of Bristol. In particular Alison Taylor, Ruth Coles, Elizabeth Lazarus, Pat Triggs and Simon Mills for allowing us to quote their work in detail.

Introduction

New technologies and pedagogies in the digital classroom

> Most people are accustomed to asking the question 'What will the new technology do?' very few are inclined to ask 'What will it undo?' Then I think we have to ask the question 'Who will be the winners and who the losers in any new technology?' because all technological innovation is a Faustian bargain – it giveth and it taketh away, but not in equal measure.
>
> (Postman 1994)

The word 'techno' derives from the Greek *technē*, which means art or skill. It is the word from which modern terms such as 'technical' and 'technique' are derived. In one sense, technology means 'knowledge of applied science and engineering'; in another sense, it means 'systematic treatment'. Yet, when we hear the word 'technology' what often springs to mind are images of powerful machines, engines, instruments, weapons and complex systems. In terms of new media, we think similarly although the objects of our imagery are somewhat different including photography, cinema, television, video, DVDs, graphics, communications, multimedia, mobile technology, the Internet and virtual-reality systems.

We cannot avoid technology if we set out to examine the notion of the 'digital class-room'. Technological progress appears to be relentless and is driven by various human needs including curiosity, and the need to solve problems quickly. There are also commercial imperatives which can result in products and technologies being adapted despite having similar functions and purposes. The field of mass entertainment is one area where much of this competition and repetition emerges, and it is an area that creates dissonance between the experiences children have with technology in the classroom and outside of it.

Technology is not a new concept. The relationship between human need and technological invention harks back to human prehistory. The emergence of the simplest stone tool was an act of technological innovation while the invention of the printing press was perhaps the greatest breakthrough of the last millennium. The industrial revolution was the cradle for much of the technology we recognise today. The invention of engines and machine tools leading to new forms of production was characterised by factories, assembly lines, synchronisation of workforces and standardisation of parts. During the second half of the twentieth century, technology began to move beyond the industrial or machine age to enter what commentators refer to as the 'post-industrial' or 'information age'.

Technological determinism

One of the defining ideas of the so-called 'information age' is technological determinism. This expression refers to the belief that technological advance is inevitable. Baudrillard (1996) characterised this process in its extreme form when he claimed that 'whole societies can be envisioned as effects of their characteristic media technologies'. This slightly fatalistic view sees technology as the main determinant despite the fact that people are responsible for both its creation and its use. The social and educational impact of new technologies, therefore, needs to be considered, as does the inference that somehow technology is neutral – ethically, politically and pedagogically. Technology is far from neutral. Television, the most pervasive of visual technologies, is heavily defined by its content, its owners, controllers and, of course, its viewers. Even photocopiers were considered dangerous in the old Soviet Union because they had the capacity to threaten the regime. It is perhaps symptomatic of the current educational era that a great deal of new technology is still greeted with scepticism because of this deterministic referent, with many teachers preferring to either subvert its intentions or ignore its potential.

Three classes of uncertainty emerge when new technology is discussed and presented as a way forward for education:

1   Teaching is known while technology is uncertain.
2   Technology is known but its application is uncertain.
3   All the signals of change are uncertain, so let's wait and see.

None of the three are new, and all are fairly typical. However, what makes them more prescient is the fact that the use of new technology requires a leap of faith and imagination perhaps greater than at any other time in our educational history. We are living in an age where advances are real and where it is not possible to impose meaningful time or probability parameters on technological change.

As a result, teachers respond to new technologies in different ways and four categories are distinguishable. First are the enthusiasts. They see the enormous potential in digital technology and try to master its complexities. They also see its use as a professional and pedagogic challenge and an opportunity. Second are the pragmatists. They support the appropriate and alternative uses of information and communication technology (ICT), are mildly critical of some of its excesses but see its potential to improve aspects of learning. Third are traditionalists who prefer to resist the advance of new technologies in schools in order to preserve a more esoteric order of learning based on human interaction and long-established pedagogy. Finally, there are the 'New Luddites' who are so critical of new technology that they seek to undermine its potential and use at every turn by seeking to undermine the profession's dependence on it.

Whilst viewing the fourth category as untenable and based on the 'revenge effect' (Sutherland *et al.* 2007), the third has a long and laudable history. However, we are of the view that given the ever-increasing presence of technology in our lives, ignoring and rejecting it are not viable options, although we accept the need to maintain a historical and critical analysis of it. We are also aware that much of the interest in technological determinism arose out of the work of Marshall McLuhan (1964). His seminal text *Understanding Media* declared the mass media to be 'extensions of man' and that new technology had enormous 'magnifying power'. One of McLuhan's famous slogans was 'the medium is the message'. McLuhan meant that the medium or the delivery system was more important than the content it delivered. Renewed interest in this area has stemmed from developments in Internet technology and the distinction used by new-media critics between 'hot' (typically the genre of film) and 'cool' (television and televisual communications) media as ways of classifying our relationship with culture. The Internet, however, coalesces these classifications through its capacity to be participatory, synchronous, situated, visual, knowledge and information driven, that is both cool and hot simultaneously.

It is, perhaps, symptomatic of our current fascination with digitalisation that we have now moved away from an overt fear of determinism to a position where we see the potential in new technology and seek to use it to our best advantage.

Computers and digitisation

The ability to download a movie clip or a piece of music from the Internet, the capacity to load an image onto your computer and then send it to others and the ability to complete these tasks on ever smaller and distributed networks of peripheral hardware (iPods, mobile phones, etc.) have all been made possible by digitisation. The shift from analogue to the digital creation and recording of images and information has transformed new-media uses and the human relations that work off them. Digital technologies are shaping the future of teaching and learning and, coupled with the vastness of the Internet, are providing teachers and students alike with unprecedented opportunities for creativity and exploration. To what extent they are actually changing classroom practices remains open for debate.

New technology and learning

Imagine a party of time travellers, among them a group of surgeons and a group of school teachers, who came from the last century to see how things are done in our days. Think of the bewilderment of surgeons when they find themselves in the operating room of a modern hospital! The nineteenth-century surgeons can make no sense at all of what these strangely garbed twentieth-century people are doing. Although they may be able to see that a surgical operation of some sort is being performed, they are unlikely to figure out what it is. The rituals of antisepsis, the practice of anaesthesia, the beeping electronics, even the bright lights are utterly unfamiliar. Certainly they would not be able to help.

How different the reaction of time-travelling teachers to a modern classroom! These teachers from the past are puzzled by a few strange objects, they are shocked by the styles of clothing and haircuts, but they fully see the points of most of what is happening and could in a pinch even take over the class. They disagree among themselves about whether the changes they see are for the better or for the worse.

(Papert 2006: 158)

As Donald Norman (1993) perceptively pointed out, in the past, technology was concerned with fitting people's bodies, while today it must fit people's minds. In essence, we need to understand and experiment with ways in which technology interacts with people's minds – human cognition. Norman's (1993) conclusion is that old approaches to learning and teaching highlighted by Papert will no longer suffice, but at the same time he recognises that the side effects of these new interactions might in some cases be chaotic. However, he is also concerned (as are many teachers) that the pervasive effect of new technologies – in particular the entertainment elements – spill over into the intellectual side of life and interrupt or interfere with what is regarded as learning, leading to an acceptance of experience as a substitute for thought.

Norman (1993, 2004) explains this by highlighting two modes of cognition that operate when thinking takes place: the experiential mode and the reflective mode. The former leads us to a state in which we perceive and react to events around us – often efficiently and effortlessly. Over time, this results in development of expertise and is a key component of efficient performance. The reflective mode is that of contrast and comparison, of musing and maturation – often leading to new ideas, novel responses and creative decision-making (Norman 1993). Although these two modes represent only a fraction of the cognitive activities that constitute learning, they are helpful as a heuristic for guiding the reader through the chapters of this book.

Both modes overlap during learning, and it is possible to have a mixture – enjoying the experiential mode while reflecting upon it. In fact, many of the arguments about the value of new technologies stem from confusion about the relative nature of the two modes. Many forms of new technology often fail because they provide reflective tools for experiential situations or visa versa (Norman 1998). What this book tries to do is to emphasise the affordances and constraints of a variety of 'new' technologies – the properties that make it easier do some things and harder to do others. McLuhan's (1964) famous remark about the message of media was in many ways a comment on affordances. For instance, reading affords control of pace and levels of engagement through the portion of text read, how well it is understood and remembered. In so doing, you can muse, ponder, question, argue, disagree – in effect, reading affords reflection (Norman 1993, 1998).

On the constraining side as Norman (1993) puts it, however, reading can be slow and difficult and often requires considerable mental effort. Furthermore, practice improves the process while the mental demands made on the reader often preclude other simultaneous activities. The material is also information-rich and engages the reader in some form of narrative code of varying levels of complexity – compare a popular news-stand magazine against a classic novel for instance. The words are also fixed and often result in private engagement until the contents are discussed in reflective debate or argument.

Watching television, on the other hand, offers a different set of affordances. Whilst reading is relatively difficult and complex, watching television requires very little practice; it is often passive and gives the watcher very little control over the pace or the consideration of the material. Its seductive capacity has led to criticism and much angst amongst watchers where reflection gives way to pure experience and entertainment (Mander 1991). Nevertheless, the powerful visual images and narrative underpinning can make television – properly constructed and understood – a powerful tool for reflection and learning. In fact, interactive, viewer-paced watching combined with compositional power can lead to high levels of reflective thought, particularly if the interaction is constructed by a creative author.

In his book *Amusing Ourselves to Death*, Neil Postman (1985) reminds us of these two contrasting views of the impact of technology on society: one described by George Orwell in his novel *1984*, and the other described by Aldous Huxley in *Brave New World*.

Orwell warns us that we will be overcome by an externally imposed oppression. But in Huxley's vision, no Big Brother is required to deprive people of their autonomy, maturity and history. As he saw it, people will come to love their oppression, to adore technologies that undo their capacities to think. What Orwell feared were those who would ban books. What Huxley feared was that there would be no reason to ban a book, for there would be no one who would wish to read one. In *1984*, Huxley added, people are controlled by inflicting pain. In *Brave New World*, they are controlled by inflicting pleasure.

The arguments running through the chapters in this book highlight the tensions vividly described in both dystopias. We argue strongly for an active engagement with learning through and with new technologies so that both experiential and reflective modes of cognition can operate simultaneously. We also emphasise the fact that digital technologies are not the panaceas to the perceived problems that face our education system. They are also not the 'quick fix' so demanded by short-term government thinking. Rather, they are pedagogical tools that can enhance many forms of learning both in and out of school. We further recognise that they can also impede learning, have negative side effects and, in some cases, detract from learning – but it was ever thus. Pedagogic technologies from basic oral discourse to the blackboard and more recently PowerPoint and the interactive white board (IWB) can and do detract from as much as aid learning and teaching. As Donald Norman (2004) comments, it really is up to us – as teachers, educators and learners – to decide on the course we take and to make the use of technology appropriate to the purposes and needs that drive our educational vision. Seymour Papert (2006) further reminds us that new technologies used creatively have the capacity to move us beyond the 'just a tool fallacy'. In his foreword to Mitchel Resnick's (2006) *Turtles, Termites and Traffic Jams* Papert highlights the failure

> to distinguish between tools (reasonably described as 'just tools') that improve their users' ability to do pre-existing jobs, and another kind of 'tool' that are more than 'just tools' because of their role in the creation of a job nobody thought to do, or nobody could have done, before.

We hope that some of the ideas presented in this book will encourage you to engage your learners in ways that are previously untried and thereby encourage them to learn in ways that have not previously been imagined. Life in the digital classroom will be different – just how different it will be depends on the decisions made by teachers.

1 Policy and politicians

Chapter overview

The school classroom is undergoing a rapid and irreversible change. One of the most powerful drivers of this change is ICT. Wherever one looks in a school, there are computers, digital cameras, electronic whiteboards and, of course, the Internet. Many teachers are asking how we arrived at this situation and what will be the implications for the future of education.

A useful starting point in any narrative about learning technologies is the manner in which they are introduced. Government funding in recent years has been forthcoming as a result of the perception that qualifications are the key to prosperity. Successive policy-makers have viewed new technologies as a fundamental component in the brokering of successful pedagogy and, thus, perceive them to be politically expedient. We begin then by exploring the policies and political initiatives that underpin the recent deployment of ICT in British schools. This chapter will enable you to:

- examine the various policy initiatives that have guided practice in schools since 1997;
- appreciate the connection between policy currents and the purposes of educational change;
- gain an awareness of the key relationship between politics and policy-making.

Introduction

For more than a decade, the UK and other developed countries have launched a series of initiatives aimed at improving education through the widespread implementation and use of digital technologies. Much of this policy thrust is predicated on the link between an improving and expanding economy – particularly what has been termed the knowledge economy – and educational innovation. To emphasise this, British Prime Minister Tony Blair, in an article published in *Newsweek* (2006), declared that the increasing digitalisation of the classroom would help to secure Britain's future global competitiveness:

> We can already see how important education and skills are for individual and collective prosperity. At every level, those with good qualifications do better than those without. On a global scale, half the increase in the annual growth of productivity comes from new ideas and ways of doing things. The fastest-growing cities in America and Europe are those with the highest proportion of knowledge workers.

At the heart of this argument is the idea of increasing workforce flexibility or what Castells (1997: 340) calls 'self-programmable labour'. This requires that all workers should have the capacity to constantly refine and redefine their appropriate skills for a given task and be given the opportunity for access to a widening source of learning and skills updates. This model of learning has moved away from the traditional 'just in case' learning, where all aspects of a curriculum were delivered, through the 'just in time' economy model of training and is now arriving at a personalised 'just for me' type provision. These moves connect to a series of ideas related to lifelong learning where multiple and concurrent careers are becoming the norm throughout the entire workforce. The European Union's Education Council emphasised the value of this adaptive capacity to continued economic prosperity when they claimed: 'Knowledge can not be expected to remain static throughout life the way it used to. Lifelong learning in the context of employability will in many areas be a pre-requisite to stay attractive to the labour market' (EC 2001:5). In the UK, the origin of this approach can be traced back to the policies that accompanied the emergence of New Labour as a defining political force in the early 1990s, one that found its apogee in the general election landslide victory of 1997. This result saw the rhetoric of the campaign transform into the first wave of policy initiatives aimed at securing the foundations for the government's commitment to digital learning. More than seven years later, in 2005, a second wave of policy strategy can be discerned. This builds on the foundations laid in the earlier wave and sets the scene for both current and future trends. In the following sections of this chapter, we will describe these waves and assess their impact on the digitalisation of schools and classrooms.

The first wave: 1997 and all that

For more than two decades, politicians of all persuasions have become enthusiastic advocates of new technology and have articulated their beliefs about its role in engendering educational innovation and opportunity. As far back as 1980, for instance, Kenneth Baker promised to provide a computer for every school, and fifteen years later Tony Blair spoke on the same theme when he commented in *A Week in Politics* that 'the future lies in the marriage of education and technology'. In 1997, this enthusiasm turned into one of Tony Blair's famous election pledges to connect every school to the Internet within five years (DfEE 1997). Much of this fervour was related to economic imperatives, particularly the need to create a technologically literate workforce. As Tony Blair put it in 1997, technology in schools was about 'helping our businesses to compete' (DfEE 1997).

The election of New Labour in 1997 has been viewed by many as marking a step change in both the intensity and impact of policy-making in terms of education and new technologies. However, in the year prior to the general election, Labour had already indicated the direction of its policies by commissioning both the Stevenson Report and an evaluative survey by McKinsey and Company (1997) on the use of ICT in schools. Reflecting a number of academic studies that appeared to point to new technologies as a catalyst for bringing about improvements in educational attainment (Scrimshaw 1997), New Labour made the digitalisation of the British classroom a priority when it entered government in the summer of 1997. This flurry of pre-election activity, combined with Tony Blair's mantra of 'Education, education, education', led to what Dale *et al.* (2004) have termed the creation of a master policy for ICT and education in the shape of the National Grid for Learning (NGfL).

The NGfL was based on the consultative Department for Education and Employment (DfEE) document *Connecting the Learning Society* which was to drive the massive expansion of ICT in schools up to 2003. As Dale *et al.* (2004) show, the NGfL as a strategy was first outlined in the *Open for Learning, Open for Business* document (DfEE 1998) which sought to connect economic imperatives to the needs of an increasingly technologically literate workforce. The key stated aims of the document were:

*   to provide a gateway to educationally valuable content on the Internet;
*   to develop an infrastructure in schools, libraries, colleges, universities, workplaces and homes to support access to the Internet;
*   to provide a programme of training to develop ICT good practice.

The overall purpose was to make Britain a centre for excellence in the development of networked learning and a world leader in the export of learning services. From 1998 to 2002, a total of £657 million was made available for ICT infrastructure and for the generic training of teachers. This was enhanced by a further £710 million between 2002 and 2004. These figures were further supplemented by £257 million from the Standards Fund between 2001 and 2002 in order to develop infrastructure and to fund the start of a nationwide installation of broadband computer connections.

The NGfL, therefore, provided the strategic blueprint for high levels of investment as schools became increasingly aware of the need to carry out the government's mandate. Headteachers in particular had to assume the task of interpreting the government's ICT strategy in a practical manner. The massive, unprecedented investment in hardware in schools in the late 1990s reflected the commitment of headteachers to the NGfL even when their doubts made them stop and think. According to Dale *et al.* (2004), head-teachers' readiness to continue purchasing equipment appeared to outweigh their unresolved doubts about the effectiveness of the government's strategy. For instance, some had difficulty in reconciling the high levels of investment with perceived gains in teaching and learning. At the same time, others felt that not to invest might be too high a risk despite continuing concerns about the efficacy and impact of new technologies. Some even saw the whole process as a leap of faith. The comments below highlight this ambiguity:

> We've thrown a lot of money at ICT . . . but I honestly think . . . at the moment it is largely a waste of time . . . I'm not convinced . . . purely and simply, the only reason I'm involved in this at the moment is that (a), because I can see a future when it's going to be different and (b), I think the only way you can work towards a future is by maintaining your confidence in your ability to cope with change.
>
> (Headteacher A)

> But I think we were very clear that was the only way we had to go . . . until we've got some way of evaluating just how much ICT is impacting. It's a fingers crossed thing . . . you just hope that new techniques and new resources are really impacting on results.
>
> (Headteacher B)

Such opinions were deeply ingrained in school culture. According to Noss and Pachler (1999) the early 'fetishisation of ICT' embedded in the policy directives led to an over-emphasis being placed on hardware provision in schools as the key indicator of government commitment. Part of the strategy was based on the NGfL becoming a 'mosaic of interconnecting networks and education services based on the Internet'. This vision, according to the *Connecting the Learning Society* (DfEE 1997) document, would help support 'teaching, learning, training and administration in schools, colleges, universities, libraries, the workplace and homes'. In educational terms, this networked vision soon became synonymous with 'teaching about ICT' where teachers had to adapt to the 'computer room strategy' inherent in the vision. The espoused emphasis on delivery (Haydn 2002) also helped create the impression that this initial phase of government input was based on 'informatising' teachers and learners. As a result, some rethinking emerged from within the corridors of power that led to a second wave of policy. It was designed to address some of these concerns as well as the creation of a more wide-ranging and coherent strategy that connected up the variety of stakeholders that had come to dominate the educational sector. This strategy was also semantically linked to the umbrella term 'e-learning', an imprecise term which, according to Williams (2005), is used rather loosely to cover the educational range of ICT including, more recently, learning with mobile technologies, digital telephones and wireless connected handheld computers or personal digital assistants (PDAs).

The second wave: the challenge of e-learning

Clearly, the first wave of policy activity we have described saw the impact of ICT being tightly coupled to national economic regeneration leading to increased international competitiveness. The strategy was one based on information delivery through networked communications underpinned by an infrastructure of in-service training and resource support for teachers to 'up-skill' during this period of rapid transition. The New Opportunities Funding (NOF) training upon which this pedagogical infrastructure was built had little connection with teaching processes that might lead to improved learning. In fact, much of the strategy implied an overlay of operation where technology was forced into current school patterns and structures through heavy investment and a belief in the inherent superiority of technology as a tool for learning.

Despite concerns, the commitment of the government to ICT as the driving force behind educational reform and improvement has not diminished. The NGfL (now the more recognisable ICT in Schools Programme) led to heavy investment in both hardware and infrastructure as well as in training and curriculum integration. As a result, by mid-2005 there were improved computer–student ratios, more blended approaches to learning and increased ICT provision across the curriculum. However, despite such positive developments, new technologies have yet to yield the transformative effect on teaching and learning that government ministers had hoped for. The second wave of government action, as set out in the wide ranging document, 'The e-Strategy: Harnessing Technology – Transforming Learning and Children's Services', set out with the aim of placing new technologies at the heart of the educational and children's agenda.

This medium- to long-term strategy document builds on the e-Learning Strategy consultation set up by the Department for Education and Skills (DfES) in 2003. The process signalled not only a continuing commitment to ICT in education but to maximising its deployment and use through an integrated strategy that brought funding, research, practice and policy into a more coherent package. The e-Strategy document recognises this with a list of organisations that it sees as crucial to the success of the strategy in the coming years. The list includes Becta (Bringing Educational Activity to All) and JISC (Joint Information Systems Committee) but also the NCSL (National College for School Leadership), LF (Leadership Foundation), the TDA (Training and Development Agency), OfSTED (Office for Standards in Education), HEA (Higher Education Authority), LSC (Learning and Skills Council) and QAA (Quality Assurance Agency) to name but a few.

The vision for e-learning set out in the document is one that can help to deliver:

- the means to empower learners;
- an education system that is more flexible and responsive to individual needs;
- a school system that values and supports the continuous updating of professional knowledge;
- more creative and innovative learning and teaching strategies;
- better value for money in terms of quality and delivery.

The document also prioritises a number of strategic action areas that are considered vital to the embedding of effective e-learning across sectors:

- supporting innovation in teaching and learning;
- developing an education workforce;
- leading sustainable e-learning implementation;
- unifying learner support;
- building a better e-learning market;
- aligning assessment;
- assuring technical and quality standards.

It is clear that such priorities and their underlying vision show that the second wave of policy processes are more wide-ranging and interconnected than the somewhat prosaic first wave. This current strategy sees e-learning as part of a wider policy landscape (Pittard 2004) that encompasses inter-agency provision designed to realise the potential of digital technologies within a system built to connect school learning to wider social, economic, participatory and sector needs. All are part of a more 'joined-up' approach to learning which ties into the DfES's main priorities. These include:

- widening participation;
- preparation for employment;
- reducing barriers to achievement;
- improving the overall quality of education;
- raising educational standards.

As Pittard points out, this e-learning strategy may look different depending on your starting point. However, 'the shared agenda is the same. It is about how ICT can be deployed effectively to serve these shared aims, and how this can be done both effectively and efficiently' (Pittard 2004: 186).

Summary

Since 1997 and the introduction of the NGfL, a large majority of British schools have made significant progress in integrating new technologies into their everyday pedagogical and professional activities. Whether this has been more than just 'a shuffling of the cards' (Goodson and Marsh 1998) is still open to conjecture. However, both research evidence and intuition tell us that teachers and students are using technology more and more in their everyday activities, and we are witnessing the creation of a more blended and integrated set of learning experiences. Many of these developments have been policy-driven, with heads and senior managers in schools cognisant of the impact that digital technologies can have on learning – both in the present and future. Several positive outcomes have also arisen out of the many advances in a range of technologies and applications that are now available to the education sector. Such progress also reflects the vision for ICT and education laid out in the various policy documents outlined earlier combined with high levels of investment and commitment.

Nevertheless, even the most committed supporter of new technology within education would have to admit that progress across the sector has been slow and intermittent. Many reasons have been put forward for this lack of progress, but it is, perhaps, with teachers that the answer may lie. Teachers remain at the core of the enterprise, and future developments will hinge on their expanded role. It is vital that we understand the challenges they face, the kind of problems they experience and the barriers that seem to limit the further integration of digital technologies with their practice.

Activity

The two extracts below are taken from the two key government documents of the last decade. The first is the Prime Minister's foreword to *Connecting the Learning Society: The National Grid for Learning* (DfES 1997). The second is extracted from the recent e-strategy document 'Harnessing Technology: Transforming Learning' and contains a foreword by Ruth Kelly, the then Secretary of State for Education.

Read the two extracts and compare both their content and language. What differences become apparent? How is new technology viewed in both? What common ground can you see?

Tony Blair's foreword to *Connecting the Learning Society*

Education is the Government's number one priority. It is key to helping our businesses to compete and giving opportunities to all. That is why we intend to lift educational standards in Britain to the level of the best in the world. This will mean making the most of technological change. Technology has revolutionised the way we work and is now set to transform education. Children cannot be effective in tomorrow's world if they are trained in yesterday's skills. Nor should teachers be denied the tools that other professionals take for granted.

That is why, two years ago, I said a Labour Government would connect every school in Britain to the information superhighway. This policy is now in place, with free connections and cheaper phone bills for schools. This will allow schools to connect to each other, and link them to all our learning institutions, whether libraries, colleges, universities, museums or galleries.

Last year, I announced that we would create a National Grid for Learning, to provide the content that would make these networks come to life. This consultation paper sets out our plans for creating that Grid. The Grid will be a way of finding and using on-line learning and teaching materials. It will help users to find their way around the wealth of content available over the Internet. It will be a resource for everyone in our schools. For example, a teacher will be able to get advice on effective ways of teaching children how to read. Pupils will be able to revise for their GCSEs or explore the museums of the world for their project work. Standards, literacy, numeracy, subject knowledge – all will be enhanced by the Grid and the support it will give to our programme for school improvement set out in the White Paper Excellence in Schools, and similar initiatives in other parts of the UK.

However, there is a hurdle to be overcome before this vision can be realised. Last year, I asked Dennis Stevenson, chairman of Pearson, to conduct an independent investigation into the potential of information and communications technology in schools. His report identified two main problems – the need to train teachers and to create a market for high-quality British educational software.

The funding for training teachers in IT skills, recently announced in the Lottery White Paper, will address the first problem. The Grid will be the tool by which we address the second problem – growing the size of the market for software. Currently, the UK market for education software is too small for many companies to invest in it. And the fragmented range of products on offer can confuse schools who have limited expertise in this area. This paper suggests possible solutions to kick-start investment from the private sector in educational services for schools, to give schools some seed-corn funding to buy those services and help them choose high-quality products. The benefits could then spread beyond schools, to those involved in lifelong learning. We have great strengths in this area – with some world-beating companies from software to broadcasting, from films to computing. We have the asset of the English language. By pioneering this market at home, we aim to create markets for our companies abroad. But the biggest difference will be in our schools. By 2002, all schools will be connected to the superhighway, free of charge; half a million teachers will be trained; and our children will be leaving school IT-literate, having been able to exploit the best that technology can offer. We believe this strategy will be good for our children and our companies. I look forward to receiving your views and to working together to make the Grid a reality.

Ruth Kelly's foreword to 'Harnessing Technology'

Our plans for boosting performance and standards across education are far reaching and radical. We aim to put learners, young people – and their parents – in the driving seat, shaping the opportunities open to all learners to fit around their particular needs and preferences.

In achieving these goals the effective use of interactive technologies is absolutely crucial and I am determined that we grasp them. They offer huge opportunities that we must exploit. That means working with all the stakeholders, schools, colleges, adult and community learning organisations, universities, independent training providers, and the Information and Communication Technologies (ICT) industry, to ensure that we deliver quality and cost effective services to all. We want to extend the variety of places where people can learn.

I am particularly excited by the idea of giving every student and learner a personal online learning space where they can store their own course materials and assignments in digital form, and record their achievements. Over time we should see the technology join up better so that this is available to learners to build on wherever they go – to further learning, or to work-based learning. And in the future it will be more than simply a storage place – a digital space that is personalised, that remembers what the learner is interested in and suggests relevant web sites, or alerts them to courses and learning opportunities that fit their needs.

Online information services open up real possibilities of keeping parents much more engaged with what their children are doing, and able to have a dialogue with the school on how they are progressing. For teachers, lecturers and tutors it means easy and efficient ways of keeping in touch, giving feedback on students' progress, and managing marking and assessment. Unifying our approach to technology means they will be able to collaborate more easily with colleagues in other institutions and offer wider curriculum choice. With more flexible e-learning resources available online, teachers can adapt the curriculum to their learners' needs and interests. Technology is the key to personalised learning.

And imaginative use of ICT should help engage more learners in the excitement of learning. Borrowing ideas from the world of interactive games, we can motivate even reluctant learners to practice complex skills and achieve much more than they would through traditional means. New technologies can attract new kinds of learners into lifelong learning. Wider access to these more compelling learning experiences will contribute to the ambitions of our Skills Strategy to offer employers better support for skills and training.

Of course as we go forward in these areas we must make sure that everyone has access to this technology. We are working together with industry to ensure an equitable solution to the potential digital divide. As we continue to embed e-learning across the whole learning process, it will blend more easily with life and work, bridging the boundaries between formal and informal learning. We have proposed an education system for 14–19 which is tailored to the needs of young people, and offers more flexible learning opportunities. Technology can be mobile. That means e-learning can come to the learner. And, as demand increases, it becomes more attractive for the digital technology industry to invest in providing access. It is our goal to work towards ICT as a universal utility, creating more flexible learning opportunities for everyone.

I am also excited by the possibilities of new digital technologies to help us develop more tailored and personalised children's services. We know that agencies supporting children and families will offer better support when social workers, teachers and professional practitioners can share information about vulnerable children. We are working to help local agencies and public services join together as digital communities, creating a more supportive and personalised environment for their citizens.

I want to work with all our partners, with education institutions, with the children's and education workforce, and with the ICT industry, with everyone playing their part. Government has to set the direction and encourage the approach, but we cannot do it alone. This strategy should help put us decisively on this road to achieve our ambition for a world in which parents and carers engage more effectively with their child's learning, professionals supporting young people and families more easily coordinate their work, and adult learners of all ages find learning more fun, more challenging and more productive.

Conclusion

We hope you will agree that our examination of the policies that influence provision of ICT in British schools has been a useful starting point. The large-scale implementation of ICT across an entire education system is complex and laden with difficulties. At this stage of the implementation, the problems lie not on the desks of the politicians but rather at the feet of those engaged in pedagogy – the teachers themselves. In Chapter 2 of this volume then, our focus turns towards the relationship teachers have with technology, and we develop our theme by examining the issues and concerns that have been expressed at the 'chalk face' of education.

2 Teachers and technology

Chapter overview

In this chapter we examine the relationship teachers have with ICT. We argue that because teachers are the prime users of technology, there is a clear opportunity for them to devise ways in which the potential benefits of ICT can be exploited. However, as we shall discover, the road to harnessing technology effectively in the classroom can be far from smooth, and the relationship between teachers and technology is often tentative or unproductive. In this chapter, therefore, you will:

- gain an understanding of some of the arguments behind teachers' relationships with new technology;
- be given an opportunity to explore these arguments in a case study;
- appreciate why some of the challenges and barriers have emerged.

Introduction

Despite the policy rhetoric, you will be aware that the deployment and use of ICT in schools remains problematic. A number of explanations have been offered for the apparent lack of widespread adoption by teachers, ranging from subject scepticism on the one hand to outright technophobia on the other. Paradoxically, it is also recognised that teachers hold the key to future developments and that without their commitment to ICT use, many of the opportunities to innovate and even transform education and learning will be lost. This well-established assertion means that teachers hold the key to the technological door and should be placed at the heart of any future change.

Trojan horse or teacher's pet?

Despite their key role as innovators, teachers have always had a love–hate relationship with technology. It can be argued that much of this ambiguity comes from the ways in which new technologies are perceived. One of the primary purposes of teaching is the facilitation of learning, and new technologies, particularly those tied to the power of the Internet, have until recently been seen to be based solely on information delivery. Early computer-assisted learning (CAL) packages, for example, were based on the behaviourist model of 'drill and practice', with the computer imposing remedial loops upon low-scoring learners and offering rewards (points) for those who achieved the desired outcomes. Obviously, a distinction must be made between the old CAL delivery systems and the new interactive technologies seen in the classroom. The genesis of this distinction can be found in the metaphor of the information 'super highway' which represented the Internet as a mechanism that prioritised speed and access. The NGfL was based on these ideas where interconnecting networks would serve to improve information delivery and administrative function. This is in direct contrast to the *raison d'être* of teaching which is about the development and aggregation of knowledge and understanding, often based on a subject or curriculum area. Teachers fear that the conflation of information and knowledge will create in the minds of policy-makers and government ministers the idea that information transmission is synonymous with learning.

Such a lack of congruence between perceived learning and the delivery of information gives rise to a number of other issues. At the core of high-quality teaching is the ability to make skilful judgements about the amount of knowledge students need, in what order it is made available and how it is engaged. Such a process requires thoughtful engagement and careful planning. For many teachers, the perception is that ICT simply speeds up access and information-gathering, forcing students to look for the quick fix. This is what Ben Walsh calls 'the Encarta syndrome' where students search, download and match their findings to set outcomes.

On the other side of the equation, the new digital age has the potential to impact massively on the way we learn. In schools, new technologies pose a number of challenges to educators, prompting them to rethink accepted verities and to deploy ICT in new and innovative ways. New technologies also challenge the very idea of schooling in the conventional sense and pose awkward questions about the future of learning as being institutionally defined. We will offer a deeper treatment of this discussion in Chapter 10 where we examine how schools are extending the traditional boundaries of their activities using digital technology. Despite the obvious problems, many teachers have taken up the challenge and schools have, at least in part, been transformed by the deployment and creative use of new technologies. From the IWB or the use of computer-based simulations, or simply the use of a digital camera, classroom learning has benefited from the creative integration of digital resources. The Internet has also introduced into the classroom a wealth of new materials and ideas previously unobtainable. In effect, not only has the world been brought to the classroom through digital media, the classroom is being taken out into the world. Finally, ICT has liberated teachers from a variety of mundane and repetitive activities so that they are able to concentrate more fully on the fundamental task of learning and teaching.

Nevertheless, some teachers have viewed such changes in a less than positive light, regarding new technology as a Trojan horse designed to destabilise conventional teaching and deprofessionalise them. Some view ICT as a costly, time-consuming and problematic addition to a profession already replete with challenges. In one survey, Preston *et al.* (2000) found that fewer than 10 per cent of teachers actually used ICT, beyond basic word-processing, and then no more than once a month. Other more recent studies have found more widespread use (Sutherland *et al.* 2004), but the evidence still highlights a fair amount of ambivalence within the profession towards new technology despite it being seen as a priority within initial training. In fact the NOF that followed the introduction of the first wave of initiatives and school investment was less than successful despite the £230 million cash injection that had been earmarked for ICT skills development.

Many of the explanations for this reluctance have focused on the discourses that surround the teaching profession and, in particular, teachers' professional identities. Since the genesis of mass education through organised schooling in the last century, a creative tension has existed between internal purpose and external function, probably best encapsulated in the two primary discourses that have dominated educational thinking – liberalism and functionalism. The former still holds a prominent position in teachers' thinking where the development of the individual within a subject or curriculum area is the *sine qua non* of education. The latter, on the other hand, places more importance on the vocational and instrumental elements of education. Cutting across the two discourses is the emphasis on pedagogy and the tradition of classroom learning as being central to all teaching acts. For many teachers, new technology is rooted in the instrumental and vocational where the learning of generic skills still predominates. Recent National Curriculum announcements have fostered a rapprochement between these two discourses (DfEE 2000); however, the tensions remain within the profession and within the basic organisational units of schools about the location, purpose and effect of new technologies and how they might operate in the coming years.

Teachers also respond to the introduction of new technology in many different ways although two typical types have become popular in the literature: technophobes and technophiles. In fact, these are probably two poles of a fairly wide spectrum of responses within which a number of in-between categories exist that reflect the diversity of reaction to the pedagogic uses of ICT.

Four interstitial response types can be distinguished: first, the enthusiasts, who celebrate the power of new technologies and try to master them in order to assimilate them fully into their teaching; second, the pragmatists who recognise the potential of new technology, who seek an accommodation with it and look to adapt and mould it to their teaching styles; third, the traditionalists who recognise the latent potential of ICT but see it as a threat to traditional subject teaching and their professional knowledge and identity; fourth, the 'refuseniks' who are so critical of new technology and teachers' possible dependence on it that they resist its use and refuse to engage with its pedagogical potential.

However, given the ever-increasing presence of digital technology in schools, ignoring or rejecting it can no longer be considered viable options. Instead, we should attempt to understand the barriers and anxieties that can give rise to the patterns of behaviour outlined above. Such an approach foregrounds evidence and the need for teachers to understand their own apprehensions through a critical awareness of why barriers exist and how they might be overcome. In the next section we will highlight some of these issues and comment on them through an imagined conversation between two teachers.

A conversation . . .

The power and potential of ICTs are yet to be fully realised in schools. Many barriers to full exploitation of educational technologies exist, including technological constraints such as bandwidth limitations and lack of hardware, political issues such as funding and regulation of activities and human issues, such as lack of knowledge and skill. It has been argued that one of the most difficult areas to address lies within the psychological domain (Wheeler and Winter 2005). Specifically, this means the attitudes, philosophies and perceptions of teaching staff. Imagine this scene at a secondary school somewhere in England. What follows is a fictional conversation between two teachers in a staffroom during a coffee break. Although it is fictional, you are likely to hear most of these arguments at some time in schools. Although the conversation is set in a secondary school, many of the issues are equally relevant to primary education. This passage originally appeared in a volume entitled *Transforming Primary ICT* (Wheeler and Winter 2005).

Activity

Read through the following scenario, and while you are doing so, think about the issues that are being raised and arguments that are being made by both parties.

Microchips or Mr Chips?

John Singleton is the newly appointed deputy headteacher at Broadfield Community School. The school has 962 pupils on roll and a headteacher who will be retiring within the next six months. Mr Singleton will be acting up once the headteacher retires and may apply for the job. In the meantime, he has been given the task of deciding what the main priorities are for next year's resources budget. He only has enough funds to finance one department adequately. The choice falls between physical education and ICT, both of which have a recognised need for new equipment.

One morning, as he is making his coffee in the staff room, Mr Singleton overhears a conversation between two of his senior staff. Jane Armitage is twenty-eight, and is the ICT coordinator for the school. She is also Head of Mathematics. She is in conversation with Roger Bailey (aged fifty), who is Head of PE. Mrs Armitage comes from a progressive educational background, which contrasts with Mr Bailey's more traditional approach, one he has successfully practised through almost thirty years of instructor experience, first in the Royal Marines and later in the secondary education sector. Listen in with Mr Singleton to their conversation . . .

Mrs A: . . . and I still say that we need more computer terminals in the ICT suite . . . we have two, sometimes three pupils sharing each machine.

Mr B: Look Jane, it's no good you banging on endlessly about computers – all the kids do is play games on them anyway . . .

Mrs A: Hang on. That's not strictly true. They do a lot of very constructive stuff, particularly online with the Internet. You ought to come and have a look some time.

Mr B: . . . and I bet they download all sorts of horrible stuff when your back's turned too . . .

Mrs A: No. Definitely not! We have special software to block out that kind of material . . .

Mr B: Hmmm. You can't be certain that it works though, can you . . .?

Mrs A: . . . besides which, when the pupils are engaged in meaningful work . . .

Mr B: Meaningful? Such as . . .?

Mrs A: Well . . . some of them are building their own personal web pages at the moment. It's really creative . . . they learn an awful lot . . . there's a lot of skill involved in that kind of project. Others are running computer simulations where they are government ministers. They can see what would happen if they had to make decisions that affected millions of people, and then they discuss these results – good collaborative stuff. They can explore and discover for themselves without us breathing down their necks!! Then there are the specialised software packages . . . take Success Maker for instance – that's great with the SEN [special educational needs] pupils. Helps them with their reading problems and . . .

Mr B: [*interrupts*] Look, in my experience . . . which, OK . . . is very limited . . . computers just keep breaking down. I can never get them to work for me. So I've given up. It's all very frustrating. Computers are . . . they're . . . electric idiots, that's what they are!

Mrs A: They only do what you tell them to do Roger. Listen . . . I can get you some tuition if . . .

Mr B: Not really interested. I've lived without computers for forty years and I'm not really thinking about starting now. I've other things to do with my spare time . . . what little I've got . . .!

Mrs A: But we all use computers every day without really knowing it. Your clock radio, the digital watch you're wearing . . . the microwave in the kitchen. They're all controlled by microchips . . .

Mr B: Ah . . . that's different though isn't it. They're useful.

Mrs A: [*smiling triumphantly*] You know, I think you're a little scared about computers . . . go on, admit it!

Mr B: [*frowns*] Not scared. Just can't be bothered. [*He thinks for a few seconds.*] Some people are a little worried about the things though. I've heard colleagues saying that there are elements of teaching that will be 'taken over' by those machines. I've always said you can't beat good old 'drill and practice' methods to reinforce learning . . .

Mrs A: Well, I can only quote from Arthur C. Clarke . . . you know, the science fiction writer . . . 2001 and all that? He said: 'Any teacher who can be replaced by a computer . . . should be!'

Mr B: Well, he *would say that*, wouldn't he? What does he know about teaching anyway? All he writes about is little green men and space travel and the like . . .

Mrs A: Actually, he is a very accomplished scientist too . . . what he's saying is that teaching is not about giving information . . .

Mr B: *Some* of it is!

Mrs A: . . . it's about facilitating learning. Getting kids to think for themselves. To get them to construct their own meaning and knowledge. Providing them with the best possible learning environments . . .

Mr B: [*laughs*] Sounds like you've swallowed a DfES circular!!

Mrs A: No, really, I think those principles are very important.

Mr B: Fair enough. No disrespect, but I happen to believe that far too much money has been spent on computers in this school already. The kids are becoming computer geeks, and . . . have you seen them lately? . . . some of them are seriously out of condition! What about some more cash for new gym equipment? We're really struggling with the old kit. We need new sports equipment – the old stuff's falling apart at the seams! We need new mats and we also have a pressing need for more outdoor sports gear. It's not fair. It's PE that needs more resourcing I'm telling you.

Mrs A: But PE isn't even a part of the core curriculum!

Mr B: Ah, but it should be though. Research is showing that if kids are fit and in good physical condition, they think and work better in the classroom . . .

Mrs A: So invest in some ICT equipment for the gym then. Record-keeping, pacing, timing, computers can do them all.

Mr B: [*exasperated*] Oh, come on, give it a rest! You can't tell me that computers can teach PE better than me!

Mrs A: Roger, you've missed the point. You can use computers to make classroom management easier. More importantly, we're using computers to get the students to think for themselves. To problem solve. To work collaboratively, and so on . . .

Mr B: I can do all that *without* a computer!

Mrs A: Well . . . Nic Negroponte, the *Wired* magazine man, reckons that in a few years people will be using the Internet more than they watch TV. He wrote that in 'Being Digital' . . .

Mr B: Well Nic Nitro . . . or whatever his name is . . . probably wrote that to sell a few more books, didn't he? I'll stick to what I know best – drill and practice. I can teach the kids how to develop their fitness and instil in them a sense of fair play. They follow the rules I give them and they learn how to play a sport and be competitive. It's simple. It's effective. And I don't need computers for that, now do I?

Mrs A: Roger, you are such an old dinosaur. There really is no way to get through to you is there?

Mr B: Gee, thanks, I'll take that as a compliment. Anyway, got to dash! Got a five-a-side to referee! [*Both teachers leave the staffroom.*]

John Singleton has listened to this discussion with a great deal of interest. In fact his coffee has gone cold. He has seen the resources budget for the next year, and has to make up his mind soon what he will be spending it on. He knows that to make sense of the very partisan perspectives he has heard, he must begin teasing out the key issues that have been made by both teachers.

Activity

- What category do you think Mrs Armitage falls into? Which category might Mr Bailey belong to? What dialogue influenced your decisions?
- Can you identify any underlying philosophies, beliefs or theories of learning that may cause these teachers to adopt their respective positions?
- What barriers and challenges to ICT seem to emerge?

Barriers and challenges

Given the ever-increasing presence of digital technology in schools, we have already argued that ignoring or rejecting it are not viable options.

A number of studies has explored the barriers that appear to hinder greater integration of ICT within teachers' classroom practice. Published studies have approached the problem from a variety of perspectives. Some studies have examined generic ICT use (Bosley and Moon 2003, Mumtaz 2000, Albaugh 1997, Butler and Sellbom 2002), while others have approached the problem from a more subject- or curriculum-based perspective (Goodson and Mangan 1995, Selwyn 1999, John and LaValle 2004, John 2005, Ruthven *et al.* 2004). Most have used a mixture of questionnaires and interviews while some employed observations and focus groups. Sample sizes also vary from the detailed case study to large cohorts of up to 300 teachers. Given this variety of sample sizes, research methods and focal points, the following findings can be regarded as both robust and plausible.

Many see the transformational potential of ICT as the prime means through which the ideals of lifelong learning can be propagated. In fact, in its recent pathway document, 'Harnessing Technology: Transforming Learning and Children's Services', the DfES outlined its strategy for integrating digital technology more fully with the educational experiences, lives and aspirations of young people and adults. In the foreword by the Secretary for State for Education Ruth Kelly wrote:

> [I]maginative use of ICT should help engage more learners in the excitement of learning. Borrowing ideas from the world of interactive games, we can motivate even reluctant learners to practice complex skills and achieve much more that they would through traditional means. New technologies can attract new kinds of learners into lifelong learning.

A recent report by Becta (2004) placed the barriers to ICT use by teachers into two over-lapping categories (see Table 2.1).

The external barriers are fairly well represented in the research literature, in particular, the lack of time, training and technical support. The second internal category is less tangible and includes issues of confidence and competence, subject cultural beliefs (see Chapter 10) and teachers' perceptions of benefit. Most of the reasons are difficult to extricate, but there is general agreement that internal issues need to be addressed first otherwise low uptake will continue regardless of investment (Ertmer 1999). John (2005) preferred the categorisation of primary and secondary challenges and barriers, suggesting that teachers move more fluidly between issues depending on levels of confidence, and personal and professional investment. The Becta study reflected this variability by adding further nuance to the explication of the barriers, suggesting that there were school-level

External barriers	*Internal barriers*
• Lack of access to resources • Lack of time • Lack of effective training • Technical problems	• Lack of confidence • Resistance to change and negative attitudes • No perception of benefits

Table 2.1 Barriers to ICT use

and teacher-level barriers that overlapped considerably with the external and internal obstacles suggested in Table 2.1.

In summary, the barriers to ICT use suggested by the British Educational Communications and Technology Agency (Becta 2004) research include the following (see Figure 2.1).

- **Lack of confidence**. Often teachers feel less confident that their pupils when using ICT and this removes or at least in part diminishes their perceived professional skill (John 2005, Dawes 2000). This challenge or barrier is often related to the amount of access teachers have to ICT in their private lives and the amount and quality of the professional development that is available.
- **Lack of competence**. This is related to the confidence barrier but is further connected to teachers' pedagogical beliefs, practices and expertise. Too often it seems a lack of familiarity with software and hardware can inhibit projects and desired use. This is exacerbated by poor-quality technology and continual breakdown, particularly when confidence is low at the outset. This barrier highlights the importance of both skills training (Preston *et al.* 2001) and concomitant mentoring in pedagogy and technology.
- **Lack of technical support**. This concern is implied in the previous two barriers because without adequate backup levels of confidence and competence will diminish rapidly (Cuban 1999). However, this support needs to be more than 'techie tips' but also connected to the type of chosen pedagogy and tailored to the style of teaching that best fits the teacher. Schools may need to consider the appointment of learning technologists within schools – staff who have both the technical expertise and the pedagogic awareness to develop and support staff.

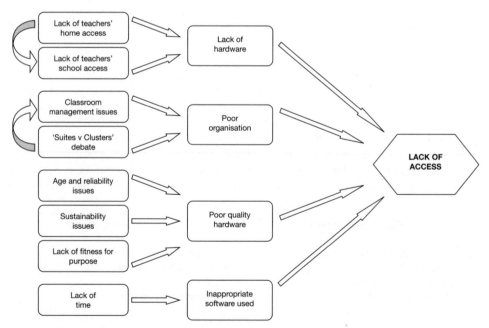

Figure 2.1 Issues relating to access to resources barrier.
Source: © Becta. http://www.becta.org.uk

- **Lack of time**. Teachers' time is always at a premium, and the Becta study highlighted this as being crucial to future engagement. Time needs to be found within existing timetables, and this should be tied to the remodelling agenda. To become confident and competent and to develop ideas using new technology, teachers require greater time for both formal and informal professional development. The international evidence is strong in this area (Cuban *et al.* 2001) and highlights the need for:

  - greater 'flexible' time so that teachers can use the software in risk free environments;
  - further modelling of learning and teaching with 'just in time' materials and support;
  - timetable restructuring so that teachers can plan how to incorporate new technology and digital materials into their practice;
  - flexibility of hardware and software allowing teachers time to experiment in private (at home, free periods, etc.) so that they can become personally 'enabled' by their interaction with technology (Becta, 2004).

Facilitators and attractors

It is clear that for many teachers, using new technology for teaching is still problematic. Many feel threatened or at the very least inhibited by its use in classrooms. However, far more important appear to be the organisational and personal barriers and challenges that can create pedagogical and technological blockages that are difficult to clear. However, as Cox *et al.* (2000) show, there is a range of positive factors that can facilitate the take up of ICT in classrooms and the perceived barriers are far from insurmountable. Table 2.2 identifies some of the key positive factors.

Conclusion

The recent DfES strategy document highlighted the importance of teachers' engagement in achieving the bold objectives set out in the plan. It pointed to high levels of investment in the education system and to the need to bring greater coherence and connectivity to the range of new technologies currently driving learning in all its forms. However, throughout there was a tacit acceptance that change would remain a pipe dream unless practitioners were enabled by the technology to bring about innovative and transformative learning across the education system. That tacit inference becomes explicit in a statement that summarises the importance of teachers to the creation of the digital classroom (see p. 95).

For any technology to work well, good teachers and tutors are required to make good use of it. This is as true of the IWB as the static chalkboard. Blended with traditional methods, or replacing some of them, e-learning allows a new relationship to develop between teachers and learners. It takes learners beyond the confines of the traditional classroom, extending collaboration and enabling teachers to bring new richness into their teaching, with learning resources gathered together from a worldwide web of digital libraries. Teachers can augment their lessons by transporting their pupils, through the use of online conferencing or webcams, into authentic environments from wildlife parks and museums to overseas classrooms. Learning of this kind extends the experience of learners beyond the traditional classroom and bring the world to the student. Lessons in this mode can provide learners with personalised and memorable encounters, and it is this theme that we will elaborate upon in Chapter 3.

Table 2.2 Factors needed for successful ICT implementation

Positive factors needed for successful implementation of ICT	*Evidence*
Coherent planning and deployment of ICT resources, ideally on a school-wide basis (PwC 2001).	Resources located in a variety of areas throughout the school. Resources allocated according to the school management plan.
Hardware and software are of high quality and compatible, allowing efficient electronic transfer of data school-to-school and school-to-LEA (Whelan 2000).	All areas of ICT scheme of work are resourced well with software and peripherals. E-learning credits have allowed software provision for other subject areas. All workstations are connected to the Internet and all classes and teachers have their own e-mail accounts.
Technical support is available (PwC 2002, Fabry and Higgs 1997).	A technical support firm is ready to come and fix any problems quickly. The phone number is readily displayed in the school office.
Training is available, of high quality, and taken up by teachers (PwC 2001, Fabry and Higgs 1997).	All teachers have had training to use the IWB in the context of their own needs and the school systems.
There is access to hardware, software and school networks for all teaching staff, and when and where it is needed (PwC 2001, Fabry and Higgs 1997).	Teachers have access to all resources both in their classrooms in the computer suite.
Successful implementation of ICT needs to address three interlocking frameworks for change: the teacher, the school and policy-makers (Mumtaz 2000).	The government has given extra funding for technology via e-learning credits, NOF training. OfSTED and the school management plan have highlighted the need for further integration of ICT.
If teachers perceive ICT to be useful to them, their teaching and their pupils' learning, they are more likely to have a positive attitude to the use of ICT in the classroom (Cox *et al.* 1999).	

Source: Adapted from Preston *et al.* (2000).

3 Personalised learning

Chapter overview

One of the touchstones of current pedagogy is the encouragement of student-centred approaches to learning. This holds true across all sectors of education. Personalisation of the learning experience is at the heart of this philosophy, and in this chapter we explore the essence of this idea. Using a number of case studies, we discuss the ways in which digital technology may be successfully employed. In this chapter you will:

- understand the origin and development of personalised learning;
- explore the dimensions of the concept;
- examine the potential of new technology to enhance personalised learning;
- study some exemplars and case studies.

Introduction

Personalised learning has rapidly become *la grande idée* of current educational thinking. Of late, it has been taken up by people of all political persuasions and parties, and, not surprisingly, it has been understood by them in a number of different ways. We could conclude that it is a concept so vacuous that it can mean all things to all people. More favourably, we could decide that its inherent complexity makes it one of those essentially contested concepts, the interpretation of which will be a defining feature of any educational perspective. Our concern throughout this chapter will not be to engage with formal definitions since these are difficult to pin down and even harder to elaborate. Of greater importance for us is the provenance of the concept and the emergence of the semantic networks that have surrounded its use. Furthermore, the potential of the idea and its close association with new technology will also be examined. We start with the provenance of personalised learning.

Provenance

The expectation of greater personalised learning has been the mantra of various policy statements since the turn of the century. As an idea, it developed out of New Labour's second term in office. It was first fully articulated in 2001 however, by Estelle Morris, at the time the incumbent Secretary of State for Education, who commented that Curriculum Online and ICT would 'enable us to move towards greater individualised learning' (Morris 2001). This was taken up by the then Minister of State at the DfES, David Miliband, who highlighted the emerging status of personalised learning as a pedagogical device. In so doing, he drew on Tony Blair's speech to the Labour Party conference on 30 September 2003 when the Prime Minister said there would be 'personalised learning for every child in new specialist schools and city academies'. Miliband developed this idea more fully in a range of speeches throughout 2003 culminating in the North of England Education Conference in January 2004 where he claimed that personalised learning is the

> high expectation of every child given practical form by high quality teaching based on sound knowledge and understanding of each child's needs. It is not individualised learning where pupils sit alone at a computer. Nor is it pupils left to their own devices – which too often reinforces low aspirations. It can only be developed school by school. It cannot be imposed from above.
>
> (Miliband 2004a)

He then went on to outline five key processes that might make this possible. These included:

1   assessment for learning that links to lesson planning and teaching strategies;
2   the deployment of a wide range of teaching methods facilitated by high-quality ICT;
3   increasing curriculum choice, especially from the age of fourteen onwards;
4   the organisation of the school, including the structure of the day and of lessons reinforced by workforce reforms;
5   links to services beyond the classroom involving the wider community including families, local education authorities (LEAs) and connected to the Every Child Matters agenda.

These pronouncements were later built upon by the then newly appointed Secretary of State for Education Charles Clarke who announced that, 'ICT transforms education and the way that children learn. Every child matters and I want a system of personalised learning that allows each of them to learn at their own pace, in ways that suit them best' (Clarke 2004). This exhortation was followed less than a month later by the Prime Minister's wider endorsement of the personalised agenda when he linked learning in education to the wider reform of public services.

> Putting the public at the heart of the public services also means services that fit the individual needs and preferences of each user. A commitment to personalised services is beginning to reverse the decades of old assumptions that the task of public service was to fit the user to the service . . . Through choice and personalisation our aim is ambitious and progressive: services fair for all, personal to each.
>
> (Blair 2004)

The semantics

The vocabulary surrounding the concept is by its nature value-laden and includes a number of aims that attempt to reconcile excellence and equality while combining high standards of delivery with fairness and social justice. Such ideas are often expressed in typical educational rhetoric with the stress on the 'fulfilment of potential', 'meeting individual needs' and the 'need to ensure high standards for all'. These broad aims are then incorporated into policy statements which focus on an ensemble of fairly recognisable mantras: choice, voice, specialisation, customisation and communication. These policy principles are often stated in broad terms and include policies that overlap with education.

Of central importance in the vocabulary is the emphasis on the learner and learner-driven outcomes. Again, the language used comes from a recognisable lexicon – one stretching back into the late 1960s. Terms include 'independent learning', 'children taking control of their own learning' and pupils 'understanding the process of learning and outcomes'. In the personalised lexicon, however, the emphasis shifts further to highlight the importance of children and students 'taking decisions' and being responsible for 'their own choices about learning'. The documents are peppered with phrases that link high standards with the creation of effective or powerful learners.

This language of effective outcomes is fairly typical of the focus on the supply side of education, in particular, the key settings. Most notably, it is those that relate to schools and colleges, in particular, the curriculum, pedagogy and assessment, and those that connect to more non-formal structures including communities, homes and parents. Again the semantics relate to fairly typical concepts: 'tailoring', 'differentiation', 'bespoking', 'flexible pathways' and 'responsiveness and diversity'. Of crucial importance is the way in which personalisation connects the different demands of learners, the variety of curriculum settings that support learning, the methods of assessment and the institutional settings that are constructed around such arenas. Finally, these arenas of operation are located within particular systems that can best foster personalised learning and include partnerships of parents and learners and the creation of learning contracts. Also mentioned regularly in the documentation and policy statements are the high levels of collaboration required between organisations and the ways in which the educational system needs to create the flexible patterns that encourage personalisation of learning (Johnson 2004; O'Leary and Parker 2004).

It is also clear that new technology is viewed as being necessary but not sufficient for the personalised learning to become a reality. Of greater significance is the interaction between technology and the learner and the ways in which this relationship is configured inside and outside formal educational structures. At the heart of the idea are the ways in which personalisation offers potential for the learner. This means that the extent of the learner's capacity to understand their learning is crucial and that new technology has the potential to provide instant and regular feedback on the basis of learning processes and products. Examples include data trackers, e-portfolios and electronic assessment, which can generate rich individualised pictures of student achievement over time. This enables teachers and tutors to be more responsive to learner needs as well as allowing each student to respond to their own learning.

A semantic web?

This potential for the learner is matched by the capability of technology to help develop various learning capacities, including the facilitation of social interaction. The age of the social web, commonly referred to as 'Web 2.0', is already upon us. Experiments with various open-architecture platforms have led to new peer-to-peer models of learning that include the use of web-logs (blogs), wikis and other variants on the chatroom. Younger children are making use of a growing number of social-networking sites such as Bebo, MySpace, Flickr and Facebook to share photos and engage in personal interactions, often outside of traditional 'school time'.

The facility to 'socially tag' digital objects such as web-page content is making it easier for students to find common interest and collaborative opportunities on the Internet. Known as 'folksonomies', this kind of fluid categorisation of digital content represents a movement away from the rigid web pages of Web 1.0 and the taxonomies of categorisation previously imposed upon Internet users. It is only a matter of time before such open-ended user-driven practices usher in a semantic web which will anticipate the preferences and needs of students, making learning on the web even easier. It appears that levels of interaction go beyond the conventional lesson time and place and become richer if students are able to access and post to shared web pages in a 'read and write' style web. This blurring of 'in and out of school' as well as the blending of the formal and the informal shows that learning moves freely across boundaries and is rarely confined to one or the other.

The dimensions

As an aid to understanding the dimensions of personalised learning, the standards unit at the DfES produced a useful heuristic (see Figure 3.1).

All the categories give us an insight into the emerging characteristics of personalised learning, and a number of clear dimensions emerge that can usefully form the basis to a more usable model. In particular, the model is linked to the wider Every Child Matters agenda and is seen as having a dual purpose: to address learner disadvantage as well as improving overall learning. In order to elaborate on the model we draw on Goffman's (1959) idea of place as a setting for action and Giddens' (1984) and Fitzpatrick's (1998) notion of *locales* as a framework designed to help understand the social organisation of personalised learning. The *locales* framework has a number of key components, or aspects, called 'individual curriculum', 'interaction trajectories', 'mutuality' and 'institutional foundations'.

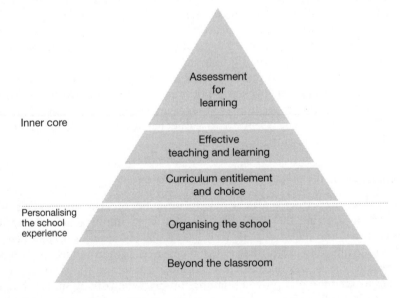

Figure 3.1 Dimensions of personalised learning.
Source: © DfES.

Individual curriculum

At the core of the idea of personalisation is the individual, in particular, the centrality of both voice and volition. In the formal curriculum, it is argued, the only choice the student has is that between competing offerings within an agreed framework. This conventional idea of the curriculum is underpinned by an institutional definition of learning. The nature of mass schooling therefore limits choice within clearly defined boundaries – often reinforced by assessment regimes and patterns of timetabling. The National Curriculum is at the core of this rigid structure and emphasises the imposition of learning norms defined by a static structure. The recent Tomlinson Review has to some extent exposed the paradox at the heart of the curriculum and state-driven educational reform by emphasising the way in which the National Curriculum marginalises the non-academic and encourages a subject-focused learning.

Prior to the imposition of the National Curriculum in 1988, the British education system was described as a national system locally defined with its emphasis on a curricular autonomy. The driver behind the reform was ostensibly the raising of standards, but in recent years this criterion has become conjoined with equity. The idea of minimum entitlement has become embedded despite the fact that a 'one size fits all' curriculum continues to be problematic. In reality, the tightening curriculum reinforced much disengagement, particularly because of its academic focus and its division into disciplinary or subject-based units. Vocational elements worked on the periphery, fearful of undermining the idea of equal access and becoming bound up with debates about selection and academic status. In fact, the manual/mental dichotomy and the emergence of an 'underclass' of low achievers disillusioned with the conventional curriculum has been a significant driver of the personalised learning agenda (Johnson 2004, Miliband 2004b).

Research evidence is useful here. In the USA, the National Centre for Educational Statistics found that the majority of students who graduated from high school found the experience largely irrelevant. However, in the state of Maine, a learning technology initiative equipped 36,000 middle-school teachers with a notebook computer and set up a more flexible curriculum. The results showed that students from all socio-economic backgrounds reported higher levels of engagement and achievement, lower absenteeism and fewer disciplinary problems. Similarly, in Germany, a personalised learning programme in Hamburg found that students' efforts in and outside school improved, and levels of achievement were also higher than those operating within the conventional curriculum.

Of course, these findings could be related to novelty, but, throughout, high levels of volition seem to be providing the key to success. This has challenged conventional wisdom while at the same time encouraging schools to offer a more challenging and relevant curriculum. It also offers a series of challenges to the assessment process which has been seen as the 'tail wagging the curriculum dog'. Much of the assessment process now operating within schools comes from a statistical preponderance of comparability and managerial data. In essence, assessment has moved inexorably away from the measurement of a child's learning towards the need to satisfy government targets and goal-setting. It is derived from a range of instruments including CATs, Yellis and ALIS. It is meant to inform macro decision-making and to provoke remedial action on areas of perceived and evidenced weakness. In all fairness, the end result is aimed at improving the learning outcomes of students, although this is often lost in the mix (Johnson 2004).

Often, this form of assessment is in tension with the more formative and 'soft' approaches taken by teachers during everyday practice. The continuous monitoring of performance, the mental note taken of improvements and changes and the everyday recording of marks, grades and comments all add to the overall picture. The accuracy of this formative approach is uncanny when placed alongside external assessments such as GCSE and SAT scores, where the accumulated knowledge of teachers is seen as being more precise than the blunt instrument of formal assessment. The personalised learning agenda should make this form of assessment more available to students and may help lever a 'just in time' form of assessment which can more readily equate to students' abilities and needs. A tension will no doubt arise with the terminal examination structure which requires a formal end date, although the increase in personalisation may, in the short term, help students to increase their chances of improved performance (see Chapter 7).

Interaction trajectories

Education, currently conceived, is still a classroom-based pursuit defined by institutional structures and, broadly, a mass curriculum. The national literacy strategy and its surrogate, the national numeracy strategy, are continued examples of the prevalence of whole-class interactive pedagogies and their symbiotic connection to the mass structure of schooling. Even the new emphasis on IWBs appears to be reinforcing the conventional pedagogies where the stress is on the structured lesson delivered to large groups of students. This collective or shared experience is central to education systems worldwide, although in many, the teacher responds differently to the challenge of individual focus. As Johnson (2004) points out this emphasis is used by the elite independent schools as a selling point where 'individual attention' within classroom-based teaching is seen as the best pedagogic solution.

Yet, increasingly, this model of mass-market pedagogy is being challenged by personalisation and the technology that underpins it. Stephen Heppell, the former head of UltraLab, reinforces these claims:

> Last century we had an industrialised model of learning and we processed students in learning factories . . . There were lots of children, so it didn't matter if each year a percentage turned out with sub-standard grades because we had plenty of menial jobs for them to do. But now most of those jobs have gone abroad or are done by robots. We need to change the way we teach.
>
> (Heppell 2007)

Personalisation is about moving beyond this approach and challenging many of its verities. To extend Heppell's metaphor, it is about moving from factory education to a more free-range model where the learning preferences, needs, motivations and abilities of students create learning and pedagogy that is more flexible and negotiated. At its heart is the idea of student agency that allows teachers to be freed from the constraints of the homogenised classroom and the 'one size fits all' approach to pedagogic interaction.

Of crucial importance to this dimension is the need to ally new technologies to workforce reform where a more fluid mix of interaction trajectories can coincide. In particular, this will require the identification of ways in which individual and collaborative forms of interaction can be negotiated to suit the learning needs of students and the pedagogic abilities of teachers. Part of this personalised pedagogy will require active intervention from teachers, particularly where misconceptions and misreadings occur. In the Economic and Social Research Council (ESRC) InterActive Education Project, researchers studying the personalised uses of ICT found that students frequently developed idiosyncratic knowledge which was often confused and at odds with agreed learning outcomes (Sutherland *et al.* 2004). This finding emphasised the need for personalised pedagogy to be embedded within communities of learning that emphasise mutuality of both learning and teaching.

Mutuality

Many concerns have been raised about the possibilities of increased learner isolation within the personalised model. The fears derive in part from the apparent similarity in individualised learning processes that continue to be part of the education landscape. Here students are guided by pre-set learning schemes that channel learning and assessment along pre-directed lines. It is also part of the differentiation process whereby students are given set options within a whole-class milieu. Personalisation, however, does not see learning as an isolated endeavour but prefers to emphasise the collaborative and mutual aspects of learning. Of central importance is the negotiation process where students, in conjunction with teachers, decide their preferred and best learning cycle and then adapt that to the mutual needs and desires of a group or cluster.

The mutual nature of personalisation is stressed in the DfES report and in the ESRC document on the topic. Both highlight the differences with individualisation where groups of learners with common features are seen as essential to personalisation. Furthermore, teaching, perhaps guided by a more research-informed pedagogy, should reflect important insights from constructivist and social-constructivist research and theory. These might include the following taken from the ESRC commentary on personalised learning:

- learning that requires the active engagement of the learner;
- learning that involves the development of understanding and the transformation of information into new knowledge;
- learning that proceeds successfully if environmental factors, which are shared by groups of learners, are elicited and taken into account;
- learning that is a process with both individual and social dimensions;
- learning that is often guided by prior knowledge and learning.

Institutional foundations

Of crucial importance to the personalised agenda is the organisational setting where personalisation promises to encourage secure foundations within educational institutions. These foundations focus in part on management systems and the ways in which workforce reform can facilitate greater support for personalisation both in and out of the classroom. Leadership is regarded as vital to the process where the use and deployment of resources combined with personal commitments to the agenda are seen as central to the securing of appropriate conditions. The infrastructure implications are clear with schools and colleges having to shift their focus away from the silo idea of educational delivery to flexible learning spaces where a blend of learning approaches can be achieved. This notion of a 'built pedagogy' will be a crucial piece in the personalised learning jigsaw.

New technologies should also be seen as central to the creation of schools as learning organisations where streamlined information systems work in combination with automated and systematised learning tools that are embedded within new learning spaces, to create the essential infrastructure (O'Leary and Parker 2004).

The potential

Much of the personalised learning agenda is predicated on the power of new technologies to drive the initiative. This does not mean that the 'computer on every desk' idea will form the basis to personalisation. Rather, ICT will offer the means by which the agenda can be realised. The increased connectivity across schools and colleges combined with the widespread use of digital technologies within conventional classrooms means that the debate now hinges on the 'how' this will be achieved rather than the 'why'. Becta's view is that ICT will be invaluable in supporting personalised learning. This will not only be in the traditional fields of the curriculum, pedagogy and assessment but also in the development of new and sustainable management and administrative systems to support learning.

Becta (2004) goes on to outline the key areas in which technology can encourage increased flexibility:

- **When and where to learn**. This includes both location and opportunity. It highlights the capacity of new technology to provide the appropriate connectivity to enhance personalised learning.
- **Whom to learn with**. This involves creating opportunities to collaborate not just with other students in the same institutional group but also with others who share interests including peers in other organisations, parents and other family members. It also means having greater variety of 'place' added to institutional styles of learning, for instance, where classes or groups from one particular institution are led or facilitated by teachers and student peers in another school or college structure.

The Becta (2004) review argues that all of the above will lead to greater choice and control with ICT being able to:

- enable an educational institution to manage its staff and resources more efficiently and effectively;
- support team teaching, team working that engages teaching and support staff in a mutual enterprise;
- provide individual practitioners with access to continuous professional development and further external expertise to extend learning within and across institutions;
- give learners greater access to external support and courses, thus improving their range of negotiable options;
- help to overcome the limitations of the conventional curriculum by encouraging high-quality distance learning;
- give access to a wide range of searchable and globally available learning resources;
- further allow minority subject or fields of interest to be taught across institutions locally, regionally, nationally and internationally.

Exemplars

In-school technology

O'Leary and Parker (2004), in a provocative paper, outline a number of ways that new technologies can be used to enhance in-school learning. The following are summaries of their suggestions for practice.

Data trackers

Data trackers are already being used in schools to encourage more diagnostic assessment and to challenge the inherent summative nature of the process. By making assessment data more personal and by providing a rich picture of achievement within a number of domains, such tools can pinpoint areas of weakness and strength and help shape pathways for improvement. (See Chapter 7 for an elaboration on this theme.) Such strategies will not only involve the teacher but also the student and other pedagogic processes. They can also help set the pace of learning as well as staged progression.

E-portfolios

These offer learners the opportunity to move seamlessly between different institutions and allow each individual to take responsibility for their completion. Their portability also encourages students and staff to engage in learning conversations at various stages and in multiple locations.

Online curriculum

New technologies also create possibilities in terms of curriculum engagement that are not limited by paper-based approaches. A live online curriculum, therefore, makes learning more than transmission and encourages the teacher or tutor to operate within a facilitating or mentoring role. This approach can be emphasised by improved guidance and greater negotiation between student and teacher where personal capabilities, personal learning styles and motivation all connect within the technology. It also frees the teacher from the chore of content preparation and delivery, providing instead a focus on understanding and engagement with the content.

Out-of-school technology

O'Leary and Parker (2004) have also emphasised the potential that ICT has to encourage out-of-school learning. Again, their ideas are presented below.

The move towards 'extended schools' represents a renewed emphasis on the importance of out-of-school experience and its impact on learning. Although based on 'added value' through extra hours, the initiative provides a number of possibilities for further personalisation. Here the potential of new technologies to integrate personal, community, home and school learning is paramount. Instead of putting the learner in a specific setting with clearly defined yet separate activities, ICT can put the learner at the core of the learning act and bring coherence across the whole spectrum of activities (O'Leary and Parker 2004).

Homework diaries

The simple act of placing homework diaries online can both inform and engage parents; it can also keep parents and carers more fully informed of progress and can highlight problems instantly. Such an approach also has more intangible benefits in helping create a culture of education which is shaped by the interaction taking place both inside and outside of the school gates (O'Leary and Parker 2004).

NotSchool

This initiative from UltraLab uses online learning designed to appeal specifically to students who, for various reasons, are unable to participate in formal school settings. This is similar to more conventional technologies that are being harnessed to create inter-institutional partnerships that allow students to gain specialist advice, guidance and pedagogic expertise. Technologies such as video-conferencing, e-mail and podcasting (see p. 35) all demonstrate moves away from timetable dominance and silo teaching.

Crossing institutional boundaries through increased personalisation also means designing and using a suite of software applications that can best serve desired ends. Making plug-ins available in various locations can be a fertile first step and might include:

- e-mail
- Office
- share point
- multimedia notebooks
- file managers
- web browsers.

A recent Joint Information Systems Committee (JISC) funded project at the University of Birmingham points the way. This initiative used an 'Interactive logbook' to allow students to create, share and amend documents in real time, thus giving them the facility to record activities and achievement for personal development. Using the affordances of tablet technology, the project allowed students to create and manage files, to view timetables, to use synchronous and asynchronous communication tools, store personal notes and materials and access other learning resources via wireless connections. This form of 'open architecture' was also flexible enough for further applications to be added as appropriate.

The 'Interactive logbook' was developed for the Tablet PC running on Windows XP but is an environment that can be used on laptops and desktop computers. The logbook's applications are located within four main sections and embedded on a screen launch panel. They are:

- programs
- modules
- meetings
- diary.

Designers claim that with minor adaptations, smaller mobile devices such as Java-enabled mobile phones can be integrated with the logbook software. Such developments high-light not only the personalised nature of the technology but also the ways in which such approaches can change the learning process. The logbook not only enhances the e-portfolio idea but also encourages informal collaborative activities and the regularity of engagement often not available to students beyond formal timetables. It also allows connectivity to a range of resources, communication and personal information while simultaneously having a significant pedagogic dimension (see http://www.jisc.ac.uk/elearning-innovation).

Blended learning

Blended approaches to education operate through a combination of face-to-face and remote learning. Blended learning has the advantage of providing students with equivalent learning opportunities wherever and whenever they are required, not just on campus. Remote learners can be connected to their tutors and with learning resources through a range of technology that can include Internet, telecommunication and mobile technologies. The appearance and features of the workspace should remain constant and familiar wherever the student is using it, and all resources and communication channels remain accessible. Increasingly, Internet broadcast techniques such as podcasting are being used to provide distance learners with learning materials wherever they are studying.

Podcasting

The term 'podcasting' is a neologism derived from a combination of iPod technology – Apple's popular media player – and broadcasting (Boulos *et al.* 2006). Most 'podcasts' are based on audio files similar to conventional radio segments. In practice, it means that digitised media files such as those in the audio MP3 format are made available on a website to be downloaded and played back on a computer or iPod. This can create a massive store of audio files which the recipient can search. Podcasting also creates individual subscriptions to a media file store via Really Simple Syndication (RSS) feed which synchronises with the recipient's computer 'pushing' unread files to the player. Recipients simply have to subscribe once initially and then each time they connect to the Internet, the RSS feed automatically downloads the new content.

Podcasting offers education a vast new mobile resource and may very easily become a simple and popular means of disseminating education content and process between schools, students and the wider community. New iPods with integral hard disks can be used to carry students' work, timetables, correspondence, reports, assessment data and communication files. In essence, they have the potential to become a personalised and portable virtual learning environment (VLE) for work in progress. They also afford a high level of personal interaction where audio files can be directly recorded via simple microphones (although a web-enabled computer would be needed to conduct basic research and communicate with tutors, teachers and fellow students, as well as create and edit graphics, text, video and most other audio files). Synchronising the player with the latest podcasts would also require a basic computer and web-enabled link (Heppel *et al.* 2006).

Despite these current limitations, an iPod can still be used to hear files and for work that involves listening and recording with complete files for assessment – both formative and summative – being subsequently uploaded for the teacher to access. Even lesson plans, with content including text, stills, audio and video, can be podcasted to students in class or remotely via a school network. Synchronising a school network with the students' personalised devices using an RSS feed means that students can be kept informed with the current class content and activities as well as homework requirements and other forms of information. Currently, the ideal would be for students to use a personal computer as an authoring device and an iPod as a mobile media device.

Case studies

Modern foreign languages

The case study here focuses on the use of an electronic writing frame produced via word processing. Using Chapelle's (2001) attempt to improve authenticity, it relied on Hyland's (2003) criteria for effective foreign language learning using ICT. These include:

- Learners are skilled users of new technology.
- They have had explicit instruction on the use of the software.
- Computer writing is integrated into the course.
- Opportunities exist for collaboration and peer support.

Authenticity, it was felt, can be improved if fluency and accuracy are supported and encouraged. Applying an adaptation of the writing frame used in other curriculum subjects such as history, science and English, teachers of German deployed the drop-down menus in Word (accessed via the Forms toolbar by clicking View/Toolbars/ Forms) as a means of supporting the aims. Within the toolbar, clicking the filed icon gave teachers the facility to construct drop-down menus behind words or phrases within a sentence. The students were, therefore, given alternative lexical and grammatical choices within a structured environment.

Primary mathematics

In order to learn about prediction, Year 4 pupils opened a Smartie tube and tested the hypothesis that there is never an equal share of the same coloured sweets. In pairs and trios, the children tested twenty-nine tubes of Smarties. They then used an Excel spreadsheet as an investigative tool. They asked two questions:

1   Does every Smartie tube contain the same number of each colour?
2   How many tubes of Smarties would I have to buy to get a fair share of my favourite orange ones?

The lesson began with a typical numeracy hour task, but as the children became more involved, the task gradually took on a life of its own. The teacher focused on the function of the charts in order to help the children think mathematically. The children began to use mathematical language associated with data-handling, including frequency, share, percentage, axis, scale, legend, etc. As the task developed, the children soon realised that Excel does not always apply an even percentage share to all sets, even if the sets contain equal frequencies.

The children then created different charts and began to realise that the more data they had the more accurate their predictions became.

Group and independent learning

An important aspect of the literacy hour is designed to facilitate small-group support so that pupils develop their own literacy practice. Below are short descriptions of digital tools which can be used by both the teacher and the learner to engage in group and independent work. Think about how you could develop these activities so that they are appropriate for the class you are working with and consider the classroom-management strategies needed to ensure that the activities maintain their focus on learning.

Writing for real audiences has been highlighted by many theorists and researchers as being a key aspect of 'good practice' (Halliday 1975, Graves 1983). Much of this work has stemmed from the ideas of Vygotsky (1978), who stated that students should be given opportunities to write for a real audience because this provides them with a real reason to undertake authentic classroom tasks while validating their actions outside of the classroom. An example includes 'e-mailing a Viking' (http://www.InterActiveeducation.ac.uk) where the changed writing style of the students was observed with interest by the class. The children were asked to 'e-mail a Viking' after exploring the relevant period. The 'Viking' was a support teacher who responded to questions put by the children. The immediacy of the strategy was accentuated by the excitement of the students as they awaited a personal response to their messages. A similar classroom-based project entitled 'e-mail an author' was equally successful. Here students emailed Sydney Northcote with their story ideas, opening paragraphs, plots and endings. The feedback to the students was quick, personal and sent from an external expert who linked the classroom activities with real-world authors. By providing a 'real audience' to critique, embellish or question work, feedback can be easily created by setting up links between other classes in the same school, between classes in different schools and even between schools in different countries.

Gamble and Easingwood (2001) claim that such examples illustrate how the act of writing has fundamentally changed. They argue, somewhat pessimistically, that '[t]he content of the message and the medium now become important, often to the detriment of traditionally important elements such as grammar, punctuation and spelling'. However, as Triggs and John (2004) suggest, the personalised feedback from another author provides greater opportunities for creative copying that can actually enhance rather than derogate the more traditional elements of literacy.

Conclusion

Other examples of using new technologies to access new audiences can be seen through the use of VLEs, school web pages and e-mailed school magazines.

The group learning possibilities afforded by digital technologies have been touched on in this chapter and will be developed further in Chapter 4 where we examine the role ICT can play in encouraging collaborative and whole-group learning.

4 Whole-class and collaborative learning
Working and learning together with ICT

Chapter overview

'Two heads are better than one', runs the familiar saying. Indeed, many learning tasks can be simplified and more quickly apprehended when two or more people collaborate. Collaborative learning is espoused as an effective method by teachers across the entire spectrum of education, from reception classes through to adult learning. In this chapter you will:

- explore collaborative learning methods in a whole-class context;
- assess the value of ICTs as tools for collaboration;
- evaluate some practical uses of ICTs in collaborative learning.

Introduction

Encouraging children to collaborate can yield dividends. It is generally viewed as a particularly applicable approach to adopt in school learning, and there are specific roles ICT can perform to promote collaboration, including the facilitation of scaffolding and the promotion of creative thinking (Wheeler *et al.* 2002).

Collaborative learning can enhance knowledge acquisition, and, when coupled with the use of digital technology, it can aid in the generation of creative thought processes through the provision of a shared electronic space within which learners are encouraged to take risks, make mistakes and think critically as they work together (Wheeler *et al.* 2002). This represents a distinct shift away from the notion of the teacher as 'information giver' towards shared knowledge approaches (Tinzmann *et al.* 1990) and a move from 'transmission' to 'transaction' (Panitz 1996).

For collaborative learning to be successful, however, teachers need to understand its mechanisms. They will then be in a position to maximise its potential to enhance pedagogical processes and outcomes. Particularly, there is a need to ascertain the kinds of learning style or study orientation that most naturally integrate with collaborative learning and to what extent some students may be disadvantaged when such methods are practised in the classroom. For the purposes of this chapter, a key quest will be to evaluate the extent to which technology contributes towards assisting or hindering this process.

In this chapter, we address these questions through an exploration of the concept of 'learning with others' and an evaluation of the educational principles and philosophies that underpin collaborative approaches to learning. We will also explore the role ICT can play in promoting this approach, and the means through which, if used inappropriately, ICT also has the potential to isolate learners and discourage productive collaboration. The chapter is divided into two parts. In the first part, we shall explore the theoretical underpinnings of collaborative learning, and, in the second, we will present some examples to illustrate how ICT can be applied to practically support the development of critical thinking through collaboration between small groups and whole groups of learners.

Collaborative learning

A good starting point for an exploration of any topic is to define it. One of the best definitions of collaborative learning is that it is a 'philosophy of interaction and personal lifestyle' (Panitz 1996). Lurking behind this statement is the possibility that those who do not wish to work with others will not benefit as much from collaborative learning activities as those who are comfortable with it. Proponents of collaborative learning argue that it enhances critical thinking through the promotion of active exchange of ideas (Gokhale 1995). The shared nature of learning within the group requires individuals to take responsibility for their own learning and this leads to critical awareness (Totten *et al.* 1991).

Teachers should be aware that children who are unwilling or unable to engage in group work – particularly those who are shy and reticent or incapable of expressing their ideas – may become passive observers in collaborative classrooms. Differentiation of tasks is, therefore, important for the teacher to facilitate. Moreover, it is possible that some ICTs can be used to actually ameliorate the above issues. Children who may feel overwhelmed working in large (or even small) groups may be encouraged to be more forthcoming with their contributions if they are able to express themselves more freely and confidently using text, images or audio and video recordings within a digital-learning environment. We will return to this idea later in the chapter.

The construction of knowledge

Contemporary views of collaborative learning are derived largely from the work of con-structivist theories such as those espoused by Piaget and Vygotsky. Piaget's premise of knowledge acquisition was essentially grounded in the child as a 'scientist' who explored his/her world independently, generating his/her own questions and hypotheses and developing expertise over time through interaction with his/her environment, particu-larly by problem-solving. Piaget's influential theory was ostensibly devoid of any social context and illustrated that successive stages of cognitive development brought the child to a new state of readiness to learn increasingly complex concepts through construction of knowledge and schema development (Piaget 1954).

By contrast, Vygotsky's approach to the construction of knowledge maintained that the social and cultural context of knowledge construction was a key part of the child's environment. In proposing his theory of the 'zone of proximal development' (ZPD), Vygotsky advanced our understanding of concept formation and knowledge acquisition onto a new level, providing teachers and theorists alike with a wealth of territory to explore in our quest to understand how learning takes place.

Zones of cognitive development

Critically, Vygotsky's work emphasised the causal relationship between social interaction and the cognitive development of the individual (Kumar 1996). In his theory of the ZPD, Vygotsky argued that all cognitive change is contingent upon interaction with others and that the internalisation of peer review defines the nature of the learning (Vygotsky 1978). The essence of ZPD is often quoted as 'the distance between the actual development level as determined by independent problem solving and the level of potential development as determined through problem solving under adult guidance or in collaboration with more capable peers' (Vygotsky, cited in Berger 1994: 241).

Vygotsky's social-cultural theory thus advances Piaget's constructivist theory of the child as an independent explorer onto a new level, maintaining that deeper levels of learning and expertise can be achieved if the child is also supported. In the ZPD, the support does not necessarily derive from the teacher or subject expert. It can also be provided by a more knowledgeable peer. This statement has significance for collaborative learning in the classroom and, as we shall later discuss, also implies a critical role for technology as a non-human 'expert' knowledge base and 'collaboration tool'.

Collaboration as a scaffold for learning

In learning, 'scaffolding' was a term coined by Jerome Bruner to describe the role teachers and more knowledgeable peers play in the ZPD (Bruner 1986). Bruner holds that as children learn, expert others support the process but gradually reduce the strength of their input over a lesson to encourage learners to take on increasing responsibility for their own learning (Tinzmann *et al.* 1990). Collaboration between the teacher and the child is, therefore, capable of generating a variable social context in which the child develops expertise in a zone of achievable competency. Within this zone, they are supported in performing tasks as they work towards expertise. Collaborative approaches can provide scaffolding for learning.

Forman and Cazden (1986) noted that children who work collaboratively often perform similar roles to those of adult experts. Collaboration between two or more learners, therefore, seems to provide a powerful route to authentic learning, but it does not preclude disagreement and conflict, and some suggest that it can be beneficial (Dillenburg and Schneider 1995). If a student is challenged by his/her peers to explain or defend his/her ideas, he/she must externalise his/her thoughts by voicing them and, in so doing, will often be required to deepen the understanding of his/her ideas as he/she talks. Students who discuss their ideas in this manner often surpass cognitive change that could have been achieved through independent study (Tinzmann *et al.* 1990). Studies have shown that learners who gain the most from collaborative learning are those who participate in this kind of exchange (Webb 1985). This kind of transaction between peers can, therefore, be seen as a reciprocal form of scaffolding.

It is also interesting to note that studies have shown that in collaboration between peers, all learners benefit, no matter what their intellectual ability. Teachers often hold the belief that in collaborative learning, less able children may not be able to contribute anything significant to the discussion, whilst those who are more able may be held back. Yet high achievers tend to gain significant benefits from collaboration with their less able peers (Johnson and Johnson 1989), and less able children are still able to contribute effectively (Tinzmann *et al.* 1990).

Collaboration as a catalyst for creative thinking

Although 'creativity' can be a problematic concept, most teachers agree that children should be encouraged to 'think creatively'. A creative solution to an age-old problem, for example, is usually derived from the problem-solver's ability to look at the problem from a new angle or to apply old solutions in new ways. Transferable skills that allow this approach are valuable throughout a lifetime of learning. For example, learning alongside peers to solve problems that are situation-based enables each learner to think creatively (Kumar 1996) using previous recollections of solutions and applying analogies of these solutions to tasks which exhibit a similar problem space (structure). Most of the problems we encounter in life have similar structures to those encountered previously, yet this is not always appreciated (Kahney 1993). Creative solutions are sometimes required to make the connection, and collaborative problem-solving in which several minds are brought to bear on the task often produces a creative result.

Mind tools and social networks

Collaborative use of technology features in several seminal education texts. Notably, David Jonassen and his colleagues have provided extensive commentary on the use of computers and other ICTs in constructivist learning environments (Jonassen *et al.* 1999). Jonassen challenges the notion that computers can be used to 'teach' by acting as a sort of electronic tutor. In the old CAL model, students were required to sit in front of a computer whilst 'knowledge' was systematically delivered to them through the screen. They were then expected to remember what they had learned and were required to provide evidence of this 'learning' by passing a series of on-screen tests. If they answered a question wrongly, the computer would send them back through a remedial loop to 'learn again'.

Jonassen is quite scathing of this approach and probably with good reason. He argues convincingly that computers have better 'memories' than humans, and humans can teach better than computers. The solution is to turn the CAL model on its head and to use the computer as a 'mind tool' – a dynamic repository of ideas, resources and learning objects which the student can use to construct an extension of his/her own mind. Mind tools act as cognitive reflection and amplification for a learner's ideas and thoughts and can aid the construction of meaning through the act of self-designed knowledge databases (Boulos *et al.* 2006).

Where mind tools are used collaboratively, a range of new and exciting prospects can open up for all participants. Indeed, it is claimed that the partnership between human and computer is now more 'intelligent' than the student or the technology when each functions independently (Pea 1985). An 'organic' form of web-based collaboration is now emerging, known as social networking. Since it was first launched, the World Wide Web was always intended to be a social environment. The web is now being used concertedly to draw people together into communities of practice, learning and knowledge generation. This approach extends beyond the traditional notion of the 'interest group'. The inception of public web spaces such as myspace.com and wikipedia.org enables groups of individuals to congregate virtually to create knowledge bases that reflect a shared and negotiated representation of expert knowledge. This is web-based collaborative learning at its most innovative, proffering significant opportunities and scope for teachers to exploit.

Wiki spaces

The use of the wiki for educational purposes is still embryonic but has been growing quickly. 'Wiki wiki' is translated from Hawaiian as 'rapid'. A wiki space is essentially an openly accessible (and therefore rapidly editable) collaborative space located on an Internet server, which can be used to generate knowledge bases. From the original concept, wikis have variegated into diverse versions including Wiktionaries, Wiki news pages, Wiki-SpecieS and EvoWiki (a user-designed and maintained encyclopedia specialising in evolutionary theory, biology and origins). Also available are Wikibooks, WikiTravelGuides and even a WikiUniversity – the latter an open-learning resource run by a research community (Dossiers Pratiques). Wikis are used by expert communities to generate and maintain definitive knowledge databases. Members of the community of practice or interest group take the responsibility to contribute, edit, filter and otherwise manage each wiki space as it evolves and grows. Wiki readers acting as editors can use a web browser to alter content, update information, alter the structure of the presentation or even in some cases rectify errors by 'rolling back' to previous versions of the wiki content. As information is organised, reorganised and presented, the user group creates hyperlinks to other associated topics or sites, and the knowledge web is allowed to grow further. In essence, the readers become writers, and the writers are the readers (Ferris and Wilder 2006).

There are, of course, the inevitable erroneous entries and occasional deliberate attempts at sabotage or false information posting, but through an almost Darwinian process of 'survival of the fittest', and close surveillance by group members, most wikis seem to maintain their accuracy and integrity. Recently, the wiki concept has received criticism due to its open-access nature and largely unmonitored web presence. However, studies have suggested that Wikipedia, for example, is at least as accurate as *Encyclopedia Britannica* and therefore has valid educational value and purpose (Thompson 2004).

There are clear opportunities to use wikis as a means to promote and support collaborative learning activities for all ages. Wikis tend to be very useful for many forms of collaborative learning but not so useful in supporting educational activity where precision is required or time is a consideration (Wheeler and Boulos 2006, Scott 2004). These self-designed databases can be used as a kind of mind tool to enable learners to construct shared and negotiated knowledge and promote active engagement in learning through collaborative research and data-gathering (Boulos *et al.* 2006).

Wikis work best for:

- knowledge-building over a period of time;
- progressive problem-solving, particularly for ill-structured problems and where several iterations of the solution are likely to be generated;
- explanation or elucidation of increasingly complex, diverse or contrary ideas;
- combining, synthesising and evaluating definitions and terminology across a range of disciplines;
- critical reading, assessment and evaluation 'in public' of other people's work and ideas;
- learning to observe deeply, and the avoidance of premature judgement.

(Adapted from Dossiers Pratiques)

Digital cameras

The introduction of digital cameras into the classroom has transformed a number of key learning activities. Digital cameras are popular because they have several clear advantages over their analogue relatives. Pictures are immediately available once they have been captured and can be quickly transferred from the camera to another device, such as a laptop computer. They can then be stored, viewed, sent, manipulated (cropped, rotated, colour balance adjusted, compressed, etc.) or printed out, with a minimum of effort. Image-capturing facilities are also increasingly available as an incorporated feature in many mobile phones, and children are very familiar with them. Picture quality on these devices has continued to improve to the point where there is often no discernible difference in resolution between digital cameras and mobile phones.

Recently, I went to watch the British National Firework Championships on the Plymouth Hoe seafront. Unfortunately, my wife could not accompany me, so during the display, I captured over thirty images of the event on my mobile phone and sent them to her as text-message attachments. She was, therefore, able to enjoy (albeit at second hand) some of the most spectacular highlights of the event. It was, she declared, the 'next best thing' to being there.

From the above example, it is evident that a number of pedagogical advantages can accrue from the use of digital cameras, particularly where a teacher requires students to work together as a team. Students need to negotiate what they will take photographs of, and the purpose behind their photography project. They can then decide which photographs are the best, most evocative or representative of the topic and which to discard. Next, they can present their work by printing these out or manipulating the images to create a montage or photo story of their project. Throughout the process, the group is corporately working towards a defined goal and calling upon their combined cognitive resources to make decisions, plan, implement and evaluate the outcomes. They will be free to defend their choices whilst challenging those of other members of the group. Further, the idea that it is acceptable to make errors and to learn from them gives the digital camera an edge over its analogue counterpart. Pictures that are out of focus or underexposed can be easily deleted and the shot taken again, with no expensive film and photo paper wasted. Digital cameras are, therefore, capable of providing a platform for constructive collaboration, and they also encourage an atmosphere of psychological safety.

Some examples of the engaging use of digital cameras in collaborative learning can be seen in the following projects:

- A teacher asks the children to form small groups and then document the growth of a plant by capturing images throughout an entire term. The teacher asks each small group to present their images in a PowerPoint slide show or digital album on a website, complete with an explanatory text.
- Send your groups out on a 'scavenger hunt' to find a list of objects related to the subject you are teaching. Ask them to take a picture of each item to prove they have found it.
- A teacher asks his/her group to create a publicity brochure advertising their local community, beauty spot or shopping centre. The group goes out and captures the images and then creates the brochure using Word or other easy to use desktop-publishing software.
- Through the use of a series of still images, or 'stop start' sequences on a digital-video camcorder, ask your groups to create a short animated cartoon, either using paper-based images or plasticine models. Organise a 'Cannes Film Festival' style presentation where each group stages a 'premiere' showing of their 'movie' to the whole class.

Activity

Design a learning activity for your own class(es) in which small groups are required to collaborate using a digital camera. Decide on the learning outcomes you wish the group to achieve and the method through which you will assess their learning. What issues would you need to address in order to ensure that each member of the group was fairly assessed?

Could this activity have been achieved without the use of a digital camera? If so, how effective might it have been?

Conclusion

Collaborative learning activities encourage learners to actively engage with learning and provide a sense of group ownership over the cognitive artefacts that result. Through problem-solving and a process of negotiation of meaning, individual learners within the group construct knowledge that can be used and adapted throughout life. ICT, in its various incarnations, can be applied to both facilitate and accelerate the process and can also provide a form of pedagogic scaffolding. In the following chapter, we focus on one particular interactive technology – the IWB.

5   Interactive technologies

Chapter overview

The number of so-called 'interactive' technologies appearing in the school classroom is rising. The use of video-conferencing to support language learning in secondary schools, for example, is beginning to establish itself as a viable and effective use of technology. However, video-conferencing has still to establish itself as a widely available technology, due principally to its high costs and complex infrastructure. Conversely, one of the most accessible and widely used interactive technologies to appear in classrooms in the past few years is the interactive whiteboard (IWB) – a device that all teachers know about and many are now coming to terms with. We have, thus, dedicated an entire chapter to this versatile technology. In this chapter we discuss:

- the nature and character of interactive teaching;
- the basics of IWB technology;
- the research evidence surrounding the ways in which IWBs might enhance learning.

'The window on the world': IWBs

IWBs are currently the most celebrated piece of new technology available to teachers and are increasingly being used to promote collaborative learning in the classroom. From early years classrooms to university lecture theatres, they are ubiquitous, providing pedagogic direction and a focal point of support to learners of all ages and styles. As Derek Woodrow, the evaluator of the government's Testbed project points out: 'It's the one piece of equipment every teacher I came across wanted to keep.' At best, the IWB can free both teacher and learner to explore new knowledge worlds while simultaneously allowing the social experience of learning to be enhanced and developed. At worst, it can be a simple replacement for traditional technologies while keeping learning rooted in the 'teaching space'. At its most effective, it can be transformative, encouraging innovative and creative teaching. As with all pedagogic technologies, however, it depends for its success on the quality of teaching and its strategic and creative use in often traditionally defined learning spaces.

The term 'interactive whiteboard' is, in part, a misnomer. Both Becta and OfSTED prefer the technically more accurate term 'electronic whiteboard' because the existence of the whiteboard does not in itself guarantee interactivity. In fact, to understand and exemplify its uses and to apprehend its potential as a collaborative mind tool, we need to start with a definition of the term 'interactive teaching'.

Interactive teaching

In recent years, the term has become attached to new technology; however, its provenance is much more complex. The *Oxford Concise Dictionary* defines the term simply as 'to act reciprocally, to act on each other'. In this sense, interaction or reciprocity of engagement is an essential part of the teaching and learning process regardless of time and place. This universal conception has formed the basis of the learning act long before formal education was established and has been of interest to anthropologists, psychologists and educationists. The concept has also been applied to various studies of classrooms including verbal and non-verbal interactions (Stubbs 1976, Galton *et al.* 1980).

In his classic study *From Communication to Curriculum* Barnes (1976), pointed out that teachers' questions dominated classroom interaction, with pupils playing more passive roles. Much of the apparent teacher domination grew out of the tension between the desire to interact and the need to keep control.

Eraut (2002) has analysed this relationship further, highlighting teachers' need to react in busy situations. In his research, he found that teachers can only prioritise their pupils' learning after they have established classroom control. Learning strategies are, therefore, accommodated within pre-existing practices. Interaction, Eraut claims, is nearly always built on this platform and consists of implicit aggregations of episodes developed from first-hand experience of particular children. These experiences are nearly always gained collectively, hence the continued emphasis on classroom interaction in the research literature and in everyday teacher discourse.

The pedagogic challenges that emerged out of the structural and curriculum changes attendant upon the reforms of the Conservative government of the late 1980s and 1990s led to a revisiting of the term 'interactive teaching'. Much of this concern grew out of the perceived need to raise standards in basic skills in order to compete with the 'Tiger' economies of the Far East. These Pacific Rim countries were, allegedly, producing high levels of achievement because of their use of whole-class interactive teaching (Reynolds and Farrell 1996). Despite criticism of this research, the basic principles were adopted by the national literacy strategy (DFEE 1998), with teachers being explicitly directed to use interactive methods in their practice. This definition was taken further in education policy and practice in the formation of the national literacy and numeracy strategies in the late 1990s. Beard (1999) and Reynolds (1998), for instance, linked interactive teaching to a three-phased framework of questioning that teachers were encouraged to use in classrooms. This included:

1   rapid recall questions to assess pupils' knowledge;
2   questions of increasing difficulty to solve an initial problem and to assess skills;
3   slower paced higher order questions embedded within whole-class discussion to help promote thinking and understanding.

This 'limited' definition, with its focus firmly on questioning, still appears to hold sway in official documentation, and there is no underlying rationale for the central concept beyond this Socratic use. Underpinning this was the desire for teaching to be 'well paced', moving with a 'sense of urgency', the implication being that interactivity was clearly teacher-led. However, as Moyles *et al.* (2003) point out, it is difficult to imagine any lesson or educative engagement 'in which some sort of pupil response is neither expected nor encouraged'. So, for them, the key term is 'extended' in that learning cannot be truly interactive unless pupils' responses are extended. The authors go further and, once again, return to the protean nature of the concept: 'Interactive teaching is therefore a complex pedagogical form and there is

no clear conception of what constitutes interactive teaching in primary schools. It is interpreted and practised differently, often intuitively in several guises by individual teachers'
(Moyles *et al.* 2003: 174). The lack of a clear definition is, perhaps, behind the desire to use
the term 'electronic' rather than 'interactive' to preface this new form of technology.
Regardless of the semantic ambiguities, we will continue to use the more recognisable term
'interactive whiteboard'.

The basics of the technology

The clearest explanation of the technology and the educational uses of IWBs can be found
at 'Techlearn', a JISC-funded centre (http://www.techlern.ac.uk). Author Stephen Brown
outlines a number of basic principles of their use – both technological and pedagogical.
Below is a summary:

Typically, IWBs are the result of convergence technologies which bring together projectors, display panels, software and electronic 'touch screens' to create a holistic pedagogic
package. The fully functioning IWB comprises four essential components:

1   a computer;
2   a projector;
3   appropriate software;
4   a display panel.

Put simply, the projector displays the computer-screen image onto the board and the
functions of the display panel are communicated to the board via the software. The screens
are then touch-sensitive through the use of a variety of whiteboard technologies including:

- **Electromagnetic whiteboards**, which are similar to traditional whiteboards in
  substance and feel. They have hard surfaces and to work interactively they need
  battery-driven pens which emit a small magnetic field detected by the frame of the
  board or by the grid of fine wires embedded beneath its surface;
- **Resistive membranes**, which are whiteboards that have a soft, flexible surface that
  resembles vinyl. They usually consist of two small pieces of resistive material separated
  by an air space to create a 'touch-sensitive' membrane. This allows the board to be
  drawn upon using a special stylus or even fingers – the stylus can also be configured
  to represent different colours. The movement of the pen or finger is dependent upon
  the pressure exerted so that this coordinates to the area on the computer monitor.
- **Laser-scanner whiteboards**, which have infrared laser scanners mounted on the
  top corners of the board that detect pen movement. To operate effectively, such
  boards require special felt-covered pens, each uniquely encoded to the reflective collar
  that the lasers use to track colour and position (Brown, 2005), (http://www.techlern.
  ac.uk).

Issues

Functionality

IWBs offer a bewildering variety of functions, and it is important to ask the following
questions before deciding which to purchase:

- Can you draw or write clearly using coloured pens and fingers?
- Can sequences of screens for playback be stored?

- Can outcomes and results of lessons be saved to the computer?
- Does the package have advanced letter-recognition systems that convert handwriting to text so it can be edited?
- Can you control computer applications via the screen interface?
- Is it possible to customise the screen appearance?

Accessibility

Synchronised software and the ability to work with a variety of mainstream and other software on the PC has significant potential for students with disabilities. IWBs, in particular, are very helpful in the teaching of hearing-impaired students and those with hand/finger touch aid physically impaired students.

Flexibility

IWBs can be fixed or free-standing. The latter have the advantage of being portable but are more vulnerable to theft and to breakdown. They can also be cumbersome and difficult to set up, due to alignment problems with projectors. Fixed boards are more secure but tend to have their use defined by their location. In terms of pedagogy, IWBs are often used for presentational purposes, but their use can also facilitate collaboration, interaction and recordability. There are also a number of alternatives:

- **Wireless keyboards**. These are keyboards that can be used to control the PC but can also be used to drive the functionality of the IWB.
- **Wireless graphics pads**. These are small portable panels that can be written or drawn on with an electronic pen.
- **Tablet PCs**. These are laptop PCs without a keyboard, and the screen can be used with a stylus. They are flexible and have a handwriting-recognition function although this is not well developed in terms of operating with the IWB.
- **IWB tablets**. These are small-scale IWB screens which work in a similar way to the tablet PC but with the benefit of reinstalled IWB software (http://www.technologiescentre.ac.uk).

Research evidence

This section of the chapter will draw on the Becta analysis of the research evidence completed in 2003 and a critical review of the literature carried out by Smith *et al.* in 2005. Both reviews used a variety of research evidence, from small-scale projects to larger surveys of use. The relatively recent introduction of the technology, however, means that a robust corpus of reliable evidence is still far from available. The impact of IWBs on learning, for instance, is difficult to evaluate, and few studies actually focus on this aspect of the technology (Higgins 2003). However, as investment in the technology grows and its use becomes more widespread, then it is likely that a more robust evidence base will emerge.

Despite mentioning the limitations of the research evidence, Smith *et al.* (2005) highlighted a number of themes that emphasised the potential benefits for teaching and learning in classrooms:

- flexibility and versatility;
- multimedia/multi-modal presentation;

- efficiency;
- supporting planning and the development of resources;
- modelling ICT skills;
- interactivity and participation.

The Becta study likewise points to similar advantages but highlights further the benefits of the technology to teachers because it:

- can increase teacher time afforded by web-based resources;
- can increase student enjoyment of lessons;
- prompts greater spontaneity;
- reduces duplication of materials;
- improves sharing of good practice;
- can be transformative.

In terms of student learning, the Becta study also emphasised that IWBs can:

- increase motivation;
- reduce the need for note-taking;
- limit cognitive overload;
- accommodate different learning styles;
- enable creativity;
- increase technological access for younger children.

A number of studies in both reviews point to the versatility of the technology and the ways in which it can be used with different age and ability groups. Various studies found the technology being used in early years settings (Wood 2001, Lee and Boyle 2003) and in further and higher education (Bell 2002). The ease of use was preferred by very young children because of the motor issues associated with the mouse and keyboard (Wood 2001), while learning in mixed-ability classes was enhanced because the screen could be split into three (Miller and Glover 2002). This ability to flip back and forth also improved concentration and targeting of task (Walker 2002).

IWBs can also rapidly create a resource-rich environment with their multimedia facilities. Integrating sound, visuals and interactivity can add both colour and interest to lessons across the curriculum. Morrison (2003), for instance, used the technology to bring history to life and to help pupils increase their understanding of the intricacies of resource material. In terms of literacy, Matthewman *et al.* (2004) showed how the multi-modal qualities of the technology helped increase interest and creativity while working on a range of media-driven resources. The functionality of the boards can also drive interest with their rotation, highlighting and zoom facilities. Teachers of other curriculum subjects, likewise, point to the functionality of IWBs as holding the key to their use. Teachers of modern foreign languages, for instance, emphasise the capacity to drag, drop, conceal, annotate and highlight various linguistic units as well as integrating visual, sound and web pages into lessons that provide the key for learning (Smith *et al.* 2005).

This ability to tap into varying learning styles combined with a multi-modal dimension allows teachers to operate more seamlessly within classes. Traditionally, lessons were often broken down into chunks or sections, each dealing with a different focus or element of learning. IWBs, on the other hand, offer the possibility of integration where the verbal, visual, textual and sensory aspects of learning are more connected. These affordances also allow a greater efficiency and urgency to be introduced, thereby changing the pace of a lesson (Ball 2003) without disturbing the 'seamless flow' (Latham 2002).

Much of the research evidence builds on this idea of 'seamless flow', claiming that the technology motivates pupils and improves their attention. This appears to have a knock-on effect on their behaviour, with some studies showing greater pupil immersion in lessons and a greater connection between the culture of the student and the learning processes being offered (Becta 2003, Levy 2002). According to Birch (2003), boys are more motivated by the use of IWBs, and teachers are also galvanised by both the potential and actual use of the technology. Some have argued for a greater participation in lessons by pupils given the functionality of the technology (Kennewell 2001) while others warn against the novelty value wearing off as the technology becomes mainstream (Miller and Glover 2002, Armstrong *et al.* 2005, Becta 2003).

Tensions

Within the research literature on ICT and classroom teaching, a series of tensions has emerged regarding appropriate and effective pedagogic use. These tensions can be described as:

*   teaching about ICT;
*   teaching with ICT;
*   teaching through ICT.

Each position represents a particular tradition and emphasis. The first highlights the importance of teaching the skills and competencies of ICT as a subject in its own right. The creation of a particular curriculum domain called 'information communications technology' is itself indicative of the trend. The second can be best defined as 'technology across the curriculum' where subject teaching is enhanced by the deployment of ICT. The third is more complex and relates to the embedded nature of technology where learning and technology are symbiotically connected. All three conceptions operate within schools – often simultaneously. IWBs appear to support a potential rapprochement because they offer the possibility for modelling skills and abilities across the whole curriculum (Smith *et al.* 2005). For instance, as Goodison (2002: 288) points out: 'Pupils are able to observe the manipulation of the operating system, the main applications and the network structure on a routine basis, so that when they come to use computers in class . . . they are fully aware of what needs to be done.'

This modelling is both a skill and a process and/or relates to both skill and process. This means that pupils can learn about the technology while at the same time being engaged in the subject discipline. Furthermore, IWBs offer greater visibility and also limit the need for repetition of instruction; in essence, they are a sophisticated aide-mémoire for the lesson structure and flow.

Much has been made of the location of the IWB and the way it can enhance whole-class teaching. Many teachers in various studies have highlighted the advantage IWBs offer in terms of 'facing the class' (Becta 2004, Smith 2001, Wood 2001). This allows teachers to make better use of the 'teacher space', thus enhancing their line of sight and improving their focus on students. In this sense, critics have argued that IWBs have reinforced traditional pedagogies by building on the conservatism of teachers. Others have responded by claiming that improved whole-class interactive teaching is necessary given the current structure of classes and schools and that collective involvement is a fundamental pre-requisite of engagement with a community of learning (Sutherland *et al.* 2004).

As the InterActive Education Project (2005) showed, learning within knowledge communities was vital if the construction and reconstruction of ideas and understanding was to develop. It was felt that IWBs did have the capacity to aid this transformation if used creatively and proportionately by the teacher (Godwin and Sutherland 2004; Armstrong *et al.* 2005). Both studies and others (Levy 2002) report that greater sharing of knowledge built from whole-class interactions, combined with opportunities to clarify, articulate and rethink knowledge and ideas, could stem from creative uses of IWBs.

Subject vignettes

Mathematics teaching

A graphic representation tool such an Omnigraph was used to add functionality and dimensionality to the graphical mode of representation. The nature of the coordinate Cartesian space has also changed as a result of the use of this software. Digital graphs can be rapidly constructed and more easily manipulated than with traditional pen and paper. They also offer the student the possibility of a whole new set of actions, including the potential to plot a series of related graphs allowing easier investigation of families of functions and their characteristic properties, a greater propensity for play and experimentation and a greater chance to investigate the effect of scale on a graph's appearance.

The use of zoom can also be useful in determining gradient at any point within a function since locally, if magnified sufficiently, most graphs appear to be straight. Both Omnigraph and the TI-83 Plus graphic calculator allow the possibility of zooming in and zooming out. Asymmetric scale is also possible (Godwin and Sutherland 2004).

Literacy strategies

These models or approaches to literacy have given rise to a range of teaching strategies that merge usefully with new technologies. Furthermore, current research has identified several key ways in which ICT can support teaching and learning whilst recognising the heuristic value of the national literacy strategy (Kress 2000, Cope and Kalantzis 2000, Davison 2000, Lankshear and Knobel 2003). They include shared reading and writing strategies, whole-class word and sentence level work; group and independent work; media studies; and reflective and plenary sessions. Each will be dealt with in turn.

Shared reading and writing

The opportunity to enable learners to read at a stage above their own ability level links to Vygotsky's (1978) theory of the ZPD, where, through discussion with a more advanced other, learners can develop their ability within an activity. Sharing texts is an important part of this aspect of the literacy lesson, both in terms of shared reading and as part of shared composition. A number of visual display technologies can enhance this process:

• Data projectors and visualisers can make any text big enough for whole-class sharing. The data projector, for instance, provides class-wide access to any digital resources, while the visualiser can make any object a shared resource, for example, the writing on the back of a packet of cornflakes, the blurb on the back of a DVD box or a section of text from within a magazine or a book.

- An additional affordance of the data projector is its ability to connect to a number of other technologies that can interact with the projected image, for example, IWBs, laptops, desktops, tablets and slates.
- Annotating text to highlight teaching points using highlighter functions, changing font colour or size can also relate directly to the teaching aspects taken from the national literacy strategy framework. Framing this around discussions about these objectives, the technology can then act as a visual guide for the learners and as a recordable map of the lesson progress for the teacher.
- Enabling students to annotate, embellish and dynamically change texts within a shared context can be achieved simply by providing students with the opportunity to share ideas with peers using word-processing technologies.

Whole-class word/sentence level

Assessing and teaching to individual learning styles (or individual approaches to learning) has been highlighted as a key way of personalising learning opportunities within the classroom. One OfSTED study suggests that '[t]aking students' learning styles into account (in this way) when planning and executing ICT lessons can greatly impact the learning that takes place' (OfSTED 2004). IWBs, for instance, can provide a kinaesthetic approach to interacting with language. Consider the two screen shots below in Figures 5.1 and 5.2

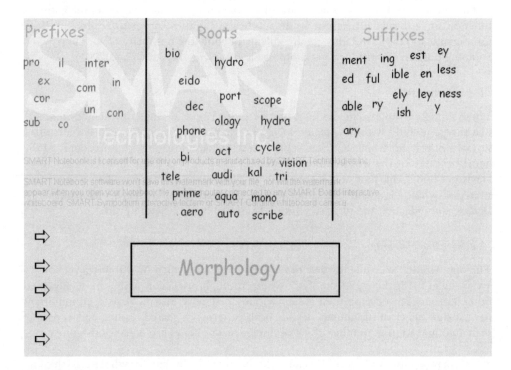

Figure 5.1 Word parts.

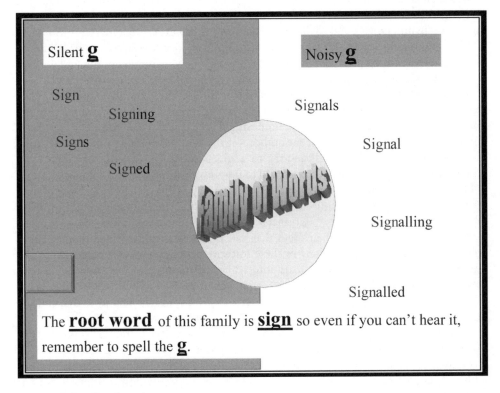

Figure 5.2 Family of words.

(taken from a Key Stage 2 classroom). Figure 5.1 shows how students can build words by dragging word parts together, before verbalising the word and explaining its meaning based upon its component morphemes. Figure 5.2 provides students with an opportunity to sort words into separate sections of the board – again using fingers (or stylus, depending upon the whiteboard). This process asks students to read the words and to sort them into appropriate sections based upon phonic principles, whilst simultaneously becoming aware of the morphological roots of the words – recognising the word family that links the word's spelling. This process was designed to highlight how phonic spelling strategies can be enriched with alternative spelling strategies to spell words with (for example) silent letters.

These examples have been taken from word-level work, but a similar approach can be taken when manipulating words within sentence-level work. Using tablet technology or an IWB allows this to become a collaborative task where students are able to share ideas whilst composing words and sentences kinaesthetically.

Media literacy

A key part of literacy teaching is developing students' abilities to communicate with a given audience. Providing an audience with a description, be it a narrative, a traditional tale or an instructional text, requires the ability to encode a message for an audience which is presented in a way that can be decoded in an accessible fashion. This highlights the merging that is taking place between the fields of literacy and media literacy. A key question remains: Does a child who can tell a story through storyboards demonstrate an ability to communicate in the same way that a child who writes a story can? While no absolute answer can be given, it is becoming clear that new technologies can and do have the capacity to transform the very nature of storytelling in new and exciting ways.

Media Stage, for instance, is a virtual television studio where the user can manipulate characters, scenery, lighting and camera angles whilst inputting their own story through speech or a text-to-speech engine. Composing a story in this environment requires a different set of competencies from the author, yet the base requirement remains the same: the ability to construct and tell a story to a given audience. The use of video is an interesting area of development that can add to the use of role play within a literacy setting.

Planning is also an important element in the organising of effective writing. Determining purpose and audience at the outset is important, allowing the student to build on these foundations through a clear organisational process. Mind-mapping software allows learners to create a concept map of their ideas that can be easily organised into themes and a coherent pattern for writing. Many of these software packages provide students with the option of changing these concept maps into a linear planning tool. This tool can also be useful in whole-class brainstorming and sorting activities. This relates back to Moseley *et al.*'s (1999: 8) acknowledgement of '[t]he capacity to present or represent ideas dynamically or in multiple forms [and] the capacity to present information in changed forms'.

Providing students with opportunities to use other methods of planning for writing can also be enriched through the use of digital technologies. Storyboarding software is well recognised, as is the use of presentation software such as PowerPoint to illustrate a story with textual commentary. This allows the students to add illustration to adorn a story as well as providing the opportunity for a range of images to be used as inspiration for a written narrative. PowerPoint can also provide different points of support for a young writer, encouraging a linear development from image as the dominant mode of communication, to image as an aid to a more competent writer. This could be used as a support structure for writers at different stages of development or to enable more detailed reflection upon components of writing, for instance, asking more competent writers to focus upon the detail of an image to aid their descriptive writing or providing weaker writers with an opportunity to tell a story through a different mode.

The spell-checker is another interesting generic tool. In the same way that the calculator is not designed to improve the understanding of division but is meant to give students the ability to calculate quickly, so the spell-checker's primary function is not to improve the understanding of spelling but to aid the performance of writing. However, there are benefits in using spell-checkers to aid the understanding of spelling as well as to support wider writing skills, for example, by giving immediate feedback to the user when the computer detects a spelling error and giving the options for corrections.

Conclusion

Essentially, when used well, IWBs add to traditional techniques and encourage collaborative involvement. Used badly, they can be as equally off-putting as 'chalk and talk' methods. However, as the literature shows, IWBs do encourage more technophobic teachers to use new technologies and help to overcome many of their fears and concerns (Becta 2003).

6   Inclusion and special needs
Access for all to the digital classroom?

> From voice recognition to virtual reality, new technologies are helping classrooms and curricula become more inclusive.
>
> (Kelly 2003: 36)

Chapter overview

Increasingly, children with special needs and disabilities are attending mainstream schools. We argue in this chapter that ICTs have an important role to play in the process of inclusion, providing children who have previously been marginalised with the *means* through which they can fully participate in mainstream education. In this chapter we:

*   explore the philosophical foundations of inclusion in schools;
*   assess the social and pedagogical impact of inclusion policies;
*   consider how digital technologies can support children with SEN.

Introduction

By implication, the digital classroom is a learning environment which potentially stretches beyond the physical constraints of bricks and mortar. This chapter will examine and evaluate how the new technologies may be used by teachers to enhance inclusive practices for pupils with SEN which are transcending the more traditional approaches to supporting learning and teaching. There is also a need to locate this discussion within the context of overarching change, both in terms of embracing the current government thinking underpinning the inclusion of pupils with learning disabilities and how the new technologies themselves are in a position to provide a highly effective tool for fostering inclusive education.

Classroom practices are the result of a complex series of processes, and many of these processes occur beyond the school environment. Recent classroom practices have been particularly influenced by technological trends. An increasing number of online resources, for example, are offering pupils, parents and educators the opportunity to engage in new dialogues and possibly shape learning even before the pupil with SEN enters the classroom. The Internet itself is proving to be an exemplary model, central for promoting inclusive practices, facilitating the innate desire of many educators working in the field of SEN to share knowledge, thinking and the practical development of resources which have been designed to impact on very specific learning difficulties. This chapter also tries to engage with this discourse by ensuring that almost all the examples of resources cited are freely accessible and available to all Internet users.

In this chapter, we present a series of reflections, case studies and key questions which will serve to provide opportunities to examine your own professional practice and examples of thinking and practice by fellow practitioners.

Inclusion in context

To many, the inclusive classroom is typically viewed as being established within the mainstream environment, where pupils who have a range of learning and physical disabilities work alongside their peers. All pupils, regardless of disability, will be provided with a learning context that exactly suits their individualised needs and, where necessary, will be supported by additional adults and resources. Most schools, of course, also provide an appropriate access to a gleaming range of sophisticated ICT equipment aimed at encouraging learners who have challenging needs to actively engage in all aspects of their learning.

However, it is important that the vision of inclusion should be seen as wider and more sophisticated than this. Rather, it is about the pupil being involved in his or her learning at all times, in a context that best suits that pupil, acknowledging that a pupil may at times be best educated within specialist provision. Inclusion, perhaps, can be best described as a series of principles (DfES 2006a) and processes (Centre for Studies in Inclusive Education [CSIE] 2002). Schools are, therefore, encouraged to evaluate their progress on the pathway to achieving a shared vision of inclusion and to identify what still needs to be addressed. The CSIE describes the inclusive school as embracing a culture which increases the participation of students in, and reducing their exclusion from, the cultures, curricula and communities of local schools.

Clearly, in order to meet the almost infinite range and complexity of learning difficulties that pupils can present, it is important to identify core areas for intervention which can help us see through the maze of barriers and opportunities that pupils with SEN can face. These areas transcend the curriculum boundaries but are integral to all aspects of learning, including the development of social skills and pupil independence. However, the implementation of the inclusive process is dependent on successfully interweaving complex thinking and practices, ranging from the macro-political to the micro-operational. The question then arises: How can ICT play a part in ensuring that the miasma of regulation, debate and experience be translated into the provision of a valued learning experience for pupils who have learning difficulties requiring special educational provision to be made for them via a broad and balanced education (DfES 2006a)?

It is possible to identify three tiers or levels through which the implementation of inclusive practices is currently being energised:

- the **macro-political operational level**, with guidance and regulation originating from central government departments, with reference to relevant focus groups and concerned agencies;
- the **micro-political operational level**, whereby schools and groups of educators implement policies and guidance from above but set within a context appropriate for their needs;
- the **micro-operational level**: the child-educator technology interface.

The macro-political operational level

At the heart of the wider political agenda, inclusion is seen as essential to achieving social and community cohesion – an opportunity for society to embrace all minority groups and offer everyone, regardless of race, creed, faith, gender, sexual orientation and disability, the same right of access to all elements of their communities. Access is the key word here. What does this mean for pupils with learning and other disabilities? Most of us would agree that the provision of access for all into education is not merely desirable and equitable – it is a fundamental human right, or 'norm' (UNESCO 1994). It is also a legal requirement. At the time of writing, schools across the United Kingdom are busy working towards upgrading their infrastructures and environs to comply with government legislation aimed at ensuring provision of access to education for all (Disability Discrimination Act 1995). Furthermore, the Special Educational Needs and Disabilities Act (SENDA 2001) has ensured that all students' special needs are supported by access to a range of specialists including educational psychologists, occupational therapists and special educational needs coordinators (SENCOs).

For most, this legislation means the building of access ramps, installation of disabled toilets, automatic doors and other essential devices. Yet, the ethos of inclusion and the Act itself go well beyond this. Educators are now required to be proactive in the way they develop learning and teaching for pupils or, indeed, potential pupils, embracing new skills which will help them understand the impact of disability on learning and develop their practice accordingly. Many mainstream schools are now including pupils who might formerly have been educated in special schools, while the latter are required to define their own pupil profiles much more specifically.

Recent demographic trends within the schools sector, promoted by national inclusion policies and targets, has meant that special schools, where approximately 1 per cent of pupils are currently taught (National Audit Office 2006), are becoming more specific in the range of needs they are expected to meet. Many such schools now have much higher populations of profoundly disabled children who are high on the autistic continuum. Yet, inclusive practices are still fundamental to the ethos of the school if we consider how pupils are being engaged in challenging but meaningful learning activities which seek to help them to achieve their full educational potential.

The rights of pupils with SEN and their parents to have full access to what is, in educational terms, their entitlement, requires knowledge and understanding of what choices, pathways and resources are available to them.

Internet resources

Central government has embraced the Internet revolution with zeal. If 'democratisation' is seen as a process in which the individual's access to information is a cornerstone (Jilani 2003), the current administration's drive to provide online access to a wealth of information is to be applauded. Within education, government departments offer a huge range of resources aimed at parents, educators, associated agencies and pupils themselves. Some are backed by legislation and others offered as guidance, although it is not always easy to discriminate between the two. Nor is it always easy to disentangle the relevant information required from the massive content that is presented. Perhaps more open to debate is the way the web can be used to deliver policy change by stealth. The onus is now on the educator to seek information from large websites such as those provided by the DfES (http://www.dfes.gov.uk), the Qualifications and Curriculum Authority (QCA) (http://www.qca.org.uk) and Teachernet (http://www.teachernet.gov.uk), rather than have the opportunity to absorb a paper copy delivered direct to the school.

Major consultation exercises are conducted online, with the obvious result of expectation that participation may be low. For example, a 2005 consultation document aimed at creating legislation around 'sharing information on children and young people', a particularly important area for pupils with SEN who may be on the registers of a number of agencies and organisations, attracted only 257 formal respondents (DfES 2005a) during its three-month discussion period.

Nevertheless, parent and pupil power have engendered a demand for both information and support which is readily digestible and which will enable them to make decisions relating to the educational options available. Websites such as Directgov (http://www.directgov.gov.uk) offer 'service users' access to very specific guidance to many educational issues, including those relating to SEN, whilst parents are clearly now able to access the minutiae of curriculum content, assessment tools, the results of school inspections and how teachers should be offering differentiated activities to their children. Perhaps, even more significantly, the exploitation of the interactive nature of the Internet to promote online dialogue is beginning to develop. The use of online discussion is enabling parents and educators to engage in conversations ranging from providing mutual support through to offering informed, professional advice.

There has been a marked upturn in the emergence of focus groups which meet very specific needs indeed, with their online presence becoming more sophisticated, particularly in the way that they disseminate research and allow for users to interact with other group participants. The Down's Syndrome Information Network (http://www.down-syndrome.info), for example, offers not only a considerable amount of freely available information, including detailed research articles, but also a range of discussion lists which are designed to support specific areas of dialogue, including one for people with Down's Syndrome and others that seek to address key issues and concerns.

There is no shortage either of centrally disseminated information and guidance relating to how ICT can support pupils with learning difficulties, cascading down to educators; the Becta (http://www.becta.org.uk) offers, in its inclusion database, advice on how specific areas of SEN may be supported by ICT, whilst Learning and Teaching Scotland (2006) provides information on numerous ICT resources designed to support a wide range of learning and physical difficulties with clear advice on how they can be used. But it is the curriculum itself that offers successive governments the chance to control what is taught in schools. The prescriptive language of the primary national strategy (http://www.standards.dfes.gov.uk/primary) offers detailed guidance on how to deliver every component of a literacy or numeracy lesson, including the language of questioning.

Case study

Polly is the mother of three-year-old Joe, who has been diagnosed as being on the higher end of the autistic spectrum. Increasingly, Joe is experiencing difficulties in coping with many aspects of his life at the local playgroup, particularly in terms of developing communication skills which would allow him to express his needs. Mum is finding that questions she has about autistic spectrum disorder (ASD), its impact on communication and the future development of her son are being answered unsatisfactorily by those around her. Feelings of isolation and frustration are beginning to give way to desperation. How can access to the Internet at least provide Polly the opportunity to share dialogue with others in a similar position?

Activity

Visit the National Autistic Society website at http://www.nas.org.uk. Locate and read the real-life stories from people with ASDs and find out what it can be like to live with someone with ASD. Also provided on this website are links that offer both resources for developing the Picture Exchange Communication System (PECS) and parents' experiences of using it. PECS is an invaluable tool for developing communication skills for people with severe ASDs.

Can you also locate a portal on the web that provides parents, carers and educators with the opportunity to discuss issues around problems faced and empathetic guidance and support?

Polly can also investigate the SEN toolkit, which seeks to provide online guidance to how the SEN Code of Practice (2001) can be implemented. Whilst this is mainly aimed at schools and local authorities, parents can use this as source of self-advocacy.

However, those pupils with more complex learning difficulties who were previously said to have been 'working within' Level 1 of the National Curriculum now have access to their own specially designed framework for English, mathematics, science and ICT, the P-Scales (QCA 2006), which provide attainment level descriptors and guidance on assessing pupils' performance. Data are subsequently collected and analysed, providing schools who have such pupils amongst their population the opportunity to set performance-related targets.

The micro-political operational level

How do schools and educators begin to manage this information in ways that promote the inclusion process, and what part can ICT play here? At the micro-political level, senior managers of schools need a clear vision of how to ensure that barriers to inclusion are being broken down, providing effective learning opportunities for all pupils. Giangreco (1997) identifies some common features of schools where inclusive education is reported to be thriving through:

- collaborative teamwork;
- shared framework;
- family involvement;
- general-educator framework;
- clear role relationships among professionals;
- effective use of support staff;
- meaningful individual education plans;
- procedures for evaluating effectiveness.

(Giangreco 1997, cited in Florian 1998: 17)

Many schools are drowning under a sea of centrally led initiatives, targets to be met, new strategies digested and implemented, rapid responses to macro-policy changes and curriculum development (Teachers TV 2006). The list is almost endless. Much of this is communicated to schools electronically, with the onus on educators to be proactive in

Activity

From your own experience of working in an educational setting, how has ICT been used to support any of the features in the list on p. 59? Consider how technology may have been used even more effectively in your examples.

the way they seek out newly disseminated information. Ironically, the same technology which is perpetrating the tide of information flooding educators at all levels can also be used to make sense of this potentially chaotic wave of information.

A core feature of ICT is its inherent property to readily facilitate the creation and management of frameworks which enable collaboration, interaction and communication. These are surely three key elements which schools require to maintain an effective pathway to inclusion. Some of the most successful ways in which technology is being used for information management are through the provision of shared frameworks for assessment and recording, using school websites as a direct means for communicating with parents and providing directories of digital resources which educators can use to support learning and teaching.

Assessment and recording are, perhaps, the most refined examples of how technology can be used to manage a highly complex process within a collaborative framework. With successive governments keen to develop opportunities to analyse pupil-performance data as a way of providing politically expedient outcomes, it is hardly surprising that they have embraced and indeed encouraged any format that electronically reports and analyses pupil (and, therefore, school) performance. Current national assessment processes encourage the alignment of curriculum content to the rubric established for reviewing pupil progress (Muirhead *et al.* 2005: 178), somewhat in contrast to the Platonic ideals of education.

The monitoring of pupils who may be working on curriculum objectives defined by the 'P-Scales' are no exception. Plymouth and Bristol local authorities have developed an assessment system for pupils who are achieving 'below age-related expectations' (colloquially known as the 'BARE' programme 2006), a freely downloadable tool which facilitates pupils' progression through a syllabus based on the P-Scales descriptors. This particular piece of software, however, has been skilfully designed to perform integrated levels of functionality. Results of pupils' achievements go beyond merely recording progress. Rather, they allow for annotation and analysis, with valuable information about additional pupil-support requirements not only being included but also able to be extracted into IEP, annual report templates and targets.

Workforce remodelling and ICT

Whilst technology has proliferated within schools, often at a rate faster than the skills, knowledge and understanding needed by educators to successfully operate it, there has been a concomitant series of radical changes to staffing structures. The traditional classroom, where the single teacher is responsible for all aspects of learning, is rapidly disappearing (Wilson *et al.* 2003).

Since 1990, there has been a steep and consistent rise in the number of teaching assistants (TAs) and, latterly, higher level teaching assistants (HLTAs), who are taking on extended roles and ever-increasing responsibility in the classroom (Parker and Townsend

Case study

Teri, a teacher working in a primary school that serves a socially deprived area, finds that the parents of two pupils who have been diagnosed as dyslexic in her Year 6 class are having considerable difficulty in supporting their homework tasks. They feel that they are ill-equipped in their understanding of dyslexia, curriculum requirements and strategies for promoting the development of literacy skills. Increasingly concerned as the two pupils seemed to be falling further behind, Teri meets with the parents and, having established that they are regular Internet users, and in line with the local authority's policy on promoting the use of a regional educational portal to facilitate out-of-school learning, sets up a community for them and their children to access. Within this secure environment, the parents and pupils are able to share discussion about aspects of dyslexia, including strategies and ideas. Teri investigated a number of useful and freely downloadable online activities designed to engage and support pupils with dyslexia, starting with those offered by the well-designed and informative Bristol Dyslexia Centre website (http://www.dyslexiacentre.co.uk).

2005). Central to the successful implementation and maintenance of inclusive processes, many TAs are more actively involved in the promotion of ICT to support children with SEN. Recent research (Townsend and Parker 2005) indicates that TAs and HLTAs are considered particularly effective when working within areas in which they can draw on specialised areas of expertise. Given access to planning opportunities accompanied by close dialogue with teachers, TAs are in a position to create content that meets exactly the needs of their pupils – frequently in highly creative and engaging ways.

Reflective activity

Jim, a HLTA working in an all-age community special school, has a particular responsibility for managing ICT and is now covering planning, preparation and assessment (PPA) time for his class teacher. Jim became concerned that a small group of Year 8 students with severe communication difficulties are behaving in inappropriate ways during playtimes. They find following social instructions difficult and can become quickly disengaged when lessons lack dynamism. With the support of his teacher, Jim planned a series of lessons which involved the above pupils in making a digital video about playground rules, ostensibly aimed at presenting guidance to much younger students and rather cleverly avoiding the idea that the film-makers themselves were to be the targets of the behaviour advice. Jim also sought to use the activity to develop the skills of working collaboratively. Over a series of six sessions, the pupils gradually took over the management of their own learning. Once Jim had shown the pupils how to use the digital video cameras and discussed ways of proceeding, the three pupils learned to assign themselves roles and to create a script and filming schedule which led to a highly successful end result: the film was of high-quality content, the target audience were engaged, and the three film-makers themselves had worked together in ways that had previously been unseen.

The micro-operational level

Assuming that the right choice of school placement has been made for the pupil and the school itself is prepared through the processes identified in appropriate policies to meet the needs of the pupil with SEN at the micro-operational level, the pedagogical considerations begin to dominate the conditions for developing learning and teaching for pupils with SEN. This leads us to pose the question: Are pupils with learning difficulties getting a fair deal and being included within all aspects of what the school can potentially offer? We, therefore, need to consider whether the school environment is providing the individual pupil with:

- appropriate access to the curriculum;
- opportunities to learn effectively;
- opportunities to develop socially;
- enjoyment, engagement and motivation;
- contented parents.

To evaluate whether these needs are being met, educators need to consider two key questions – whether these are being addressed in planning, preparation, thinking and practice and how the intrinsic nature of technology can actually help pupils have their needs met even more effectively.

1   Are we fully involving pupils in their learning?
2   How independent can we enable our pupils to become?

Are we fully involving pupils in their learning?

Recent studies focusing on the computer as a 'flexible friend' (Waite *et al.* 2007) examined the flexibility of the computer in a Year 6 classroom, with particular reference to the many individual needs observed. The personal networked computer was shown to promote opportunities for differentiation at both the physical and cognitive levels of engagement. Using a computer with appropriate software installed (for example, Movie Maker – software which is found on all Microsoft Office XP packages) can open up many exciting new ways to unleash creative thought into action. Children who are otherwise unable to express themselves can suddenly transform into creative communicators when the appropriate software and hardware is made available.

Peripheral devices are also adaptable to meet the specific and individual needs of children. Overlay keyboards can be provided so that children who have particular difficulties with letter identification can find the keys more easily, thereby helping them to concentrate more on the meaning and direction of what they are writing than on the basic mechanics of constructing words and sentences. Trackerballs and large joysticks can also be provided for children who find difficulties with fine motor control. These are superior devices to the standard mouse for their special needs.

These are essential considerations if pupils are to be fully involved in their learning. In terms of physical access to the computer, it is important to consider what interface is the most appropriate for a pupil with fine or gross motor difficulties. The provision of the standard keyboard as the key access interface assumes that users have, or are developing, not only considerable levels of fine motor skills but also a considerable degree of literacy in terms of letter recognition and the ability to organise text. This can be too much information for many pupils with learning difficulties to assimilate, and the keyboard itself can provide a major obstacle for pupils with SEN (Kelly 2003: 37).

Whilst the teaching of keyboard skills is essential for most pupils of the mainstream 'IT generation', the range of alternative ways of accessing the computer available need to be considered. Adaptive technologies such as touch screens, switches, voice-recognition software, overlay keyboards, symbol processors and screen readers are enabling many pupils with complex and challenging difficulties to engage with computer-based activities, and, whilst potentially expensive, can we really put a price on equipment which may possibly be allowing pupils to communicate for the first time?

Opportunities to adapt and differentiate the curriculum content fit squarely with the DfES's 'Personalised Learning' initiative, which describes this approach to education as a 'philosophy' (DfES 2006b). There are three key areas in which ICT can offer differentiated learning experiences for the pupil:

Learning styles

Learning styles involve production of resources that address a pupil's preferred or dominant learning style. ICT has the capacity to offer a variety of sophisticated presentation formats, based upon its multi-modality capabilities.

Case study

Helen, a class teacher of Year 5 pupils in a mainstream primary school, has recently had Jack, a pupil with visual impairment, join the class. Jack can identify blocks of colour and large fonts on the screen but has very considerable difficulty in reading the text on Internet sites. Whilst he has full-time support from a TA, Helen, working collaboratively with the TA, has sought to decrease his dependence on adult support by developing the use of screen-reading software. Jack is now able to follow the verbally interpreted instructions on an excellent numeracy education website and carry out several of the prescribed activities independently.

Teaching styles

Teaching styles are the creation of scenarios which enable students to use ICT in ways that can encourage problem-solving, investigation, experimentation, hypothesising and collaborative learning.

Case study

Jo, a teacher of Year 4 pupils with severe learning difficulties in a community special school, is encouraging pupils to develop skills in working collaboratively through the use of ICT. In this term's science unit, the pupils are studying 'keeping warm', a QCA scheme of work. Realising that many of the suggested activities are beyond the scope of individual pupils, she identifies teams of students who can, working together, carry out directed tasks between them. She carefully devises a planning sheet in which very specific and appropriate roles for the individual pupils are identified. During one particular experiment, focused around investigating the effects of insulation, one pupil has the responsibility for using the digital still camera to record what actually happened. A more able pupil had been trained in the use of a data-logger and was able to record temperatures at set intervals of the insulated material as it cooled. A third member of the group used Makaton symbols on an on-screen grid to transcribe some basic facts about what happened during the experiment. The outcome that the team provided from this activity went far beyond what any individual member could achieve.

Depth of learning experience

What is the level at which we are actually expecting the child to engage with the task presented? At the more complex and severe level of difficulty, the teacher may be aiming for a response from a particular pupil to an imposed experience, but we need to consider how we can move pupils' achievements, for those who are capable, towards the higher order skills of generalisation and application.

Case study

Sam, a Year 6 pupil who has profound and multiple learning difficulties (PMLD), has very unpredictable responses to external stimuli. Peter, his teacher, has been seeking to develop Sam's skills at being able to attach meaning to the environment around him as part of a long-term goal of enabling him to express positive or negative feelings as appropriate and, perhaps, eventually to make a degree of choice. Peter visits the NGfL's freely downloadable resources for pupils with PMLD (http://www. portal.northerngrid.org), which provide simple but engaging on-screen activities designed to elicit responses from such pupils. Sam starts to show an engagement with the simple animations and sounds which Peter has projected onto an IWB, located at floor level so that Sam can lie comfortably in front of the large image. Peter records in detail any evidence of responses made to the different resources and begins to identify aspects of body language, vocalisations and head movement which may possibly be indicators of engagement and, indeed, preference.

Regardless of the area of learning that is being developed, the ability of children to be able to communicate their understanding of, and engagement with, the world around them must be paramount. The use of symbol-processing software has made a revolutionary contribution (Pavely 1999: 44, Townsend 2005: 94) to the ability of pupils with severe communication difficulties to engage in dialogue written and spoken, with their teachers, family and peers.

Rebus, Makaton and PCS symbol libraries are now finding their way into mainstream schools, having been the bedrock of many special schools' total communication policies. Not only can these serve as a system of reading support, substituting text for a graphic representation of language, particularly in terms of providing social narrative construction, but they can, when operated within the appropriate software framework, offer students the opportunity to transfer their thinking to paper.

The publication of recent strategies to help support pupils with literacy difficulties (Primary National Strategy 2006) also reflects new thinking in the way that reading and writing skills can be supported by engaging pupils in approaches which have been derived from an understanding of how technology can help to support in other ways the development of such skills, instead of working from a beginning point to an end point. This is a particular difficulty demonstrated by many pupils with SEN. The pupil can be encouraged to gather, organise and present materials in non-linear ways which focus on developing other skills yet produce an outcome which is coherent.

The model for doing this is clearly based on use of the Internet, where pupils are able to navigate through information via hyperlinks, not necessarily sequentially, to obtain what they are seeking. Text created and read by the pupil can be used to emulate this system of operation, with files of text, video, narration, sounds and images linked in ways that encourage users to investigate their way through sections of information which have been developed by the pupil at a level which is appropriate for his or her ability level. No longer is it necessary for the student to rely solely on the ability to compose freely written text to produce a story, for example. Instead, the learner can focus on different sections, such as characterisation, and use other media to 'bring to life' his or her ideas, which are then linked to other elements of the storyline.

Whilst the software often used is not innovative, the way it can be developed most certainly is. An example of a resource which employs this non-linear approach to reading and writing, and which is proving to be particularly successful, the Social and Emotional Aspects of Learning (SEAL) project initiated by the DfES (2005) offers a number of freely downloadable resources designed to engage pupils by encouraging an investigative approach to learning. The use of familiar presentation software here as a universal 'creative platform' adapts particularly well to a non-linear narrative, with examples of real-life scenarios being presented in a format that encourages interactivity, discussion and debate within the whole curriculum framework for teaching social, emotional and behavioural skills. Equally significantly, the ethos of the Internet as a tool for fostering collaboration and the sharing of resources is further demonstrated by the availability of templates on the website which can be downloaded and edited by educators in order to provide further resources.

As part of the involvement process, are we also able to effectively promote self-determination or self-advocacy for pupils with SEN? 'Choice' is, perhaps, the defining word of contemporary culture, certainly in terms of public-services provision, and it is generally believed that the more choice there is, the more advantaged we are as citizens. The DfES cites pupils' learning journeys as ones that involve a combination of entitlement and choice. In 2005, a White Paper was published entitled 'Higher Standards, Better Schools for All: More Choice for Parents and Pupils'. However, in an increasingly complex environment, where choice is becoming ever wider, how is the pupil with learning disabilities supported in gaining access to the opportunities and choices he or she is entitled to? Rose (in Tilstone *et al.*: 95) also describes the commitment to involving pupils in the planning and management of their own learning as being implicit in the philosophy of inclusion and, indeed, central to the ethos of the SEN Code of Practice

(2001). Rose (1998: 103) identified key areas essential to successful pupil involvement, which those with learning difficulties are likely to find difficult to achieve:

- making choices;
- negotiation;
- prediction;
- sharing ideas with others;
- communicating effectively.

Key life decisions, such as transition between key educational phases, complex and challenging for all, are certainly very significant barriers for these students, but the increasing understanding of how ICT can be used to address these fundamental 'rights' is enabling many students to move forward in some, if not all, of the above areas.

Activity

How might ICT be used to address one of the above five key areas for a pupil who has learning difficulties in your educational setting in a way which promotes the skills of self-advocacy for that pupil?

Case study

Tom is a sixteen-year-old pupil with Down's Syndrome who is taught within a mainstream secondary-school setting. He experiences considerable difficulties in all aspects of literacy but has an effective, if telegraphic, use of verbal language to communicate his needs and choices. However, he is now being faced by the biggest challenge to his educational career, namely, undertaking the transition to further education. His tutor at school, and parents, are especially keen that Tom is involved in decisions around which further-education establishment he should attend, based upon a real understanding of what will be happening in the near future, as well as developing the skills that Tom needs to ask questions and communicate his decisions.

A series of visits to three local colleges was arranged. Tom and his teacher made short video clips and digital photographs of the key personnel and students he would be working with and recorded Tom's thoughts using a pictorial questionnaire format. Back in school, Tom's teacher set up a communication frame using a piece of freely downloadable mind-mapping software. With some adult help, Tom started developing his mind map, which enabled him to insert a variety of media, including the video clips, text notes and added narration, but, more importantly, it helped to reinforce his impressions from the visit and to categorise his ideas, concerns and preferences. The mind map was also printed out at each stage of the process, providing Tom with a hard copy to take home and discuss with his parents.

Automaticity and provisionality

The 'digital natives' – the IT literate generation now emerging from the education system – are generally acknowledged as having an innate aptitude for embracing the new technological literacies (Prensky 2001). The readiness and, indeed, ability to engage in electronic media without necessarily having evolved sophisticated computing skills, including basic keyboard skills, reflects the benefits that key features of computers offer us. Two key features are widely reported upon. These are automaticity and provisionality. Automaticity is a feature often used within the context of handwriting skills which is equally applicable to the computer's operation. It ensures that the most complex of technical frameworks responds immediately to the smallest of interventions, enabling, for example, a pupil with severe literacy difficulties to create phrases with meaning by placing the pointer over a ready-assembled word bank rather than expending very considerable amounts of time and energy in acquiring the most basic of handwriting or typing skills. The provisional nature of ICT will also enable pupils to experiment with confidence, knowing that any mistakes can be undone or, indeed, edited at a future date, rather than having to erase or redraft whole sections of work.

It is the ability to develop skills for engaging with the new literacies that will certainly extend pupils with SEN, and their teachers, and, indeed, may not even form part of their taught curriculum. If pupils with learning difficulties are to be included fully in not just the digital classroom but also the online global community, how can we enable them to access these new literacies?

Activity

Consider how a pupil with SEN whom you work with might develop *one* of these new literacy skills:

- **Technological literacy**: skills for accessing technology.
- **Information literacy**: the ability to gather/organise/evaluate web-based information.
- **Media literacy**: creating and distributing resources which meet the needs of various audiences.
- **Global literacy**: understanding interdependence and collaboration processes offered by the World Wide Web.
- **Literacy with responsibility**: social consequences of communicating with an unseen and unknown audience.

How independent can we enable our pupils to become?

The nature of special needs implies that the more severe or complex the learning difficulties experienced by a pupil, the more challenging it will be to develop opportunities for gaining learning and social independence. It is also very possible that the 'learning gap' between many pupils with more complex levels of difficulty and their mainstream peers will become greater as they become older (Audit Commission 2006). We also need to consider what is important for learning and what outcomes are realistic for pupils to achieve without support.

Clearly, as the child matures, expectations for engagement in activities without direct support increase. These expectations may not be fulfilled with the pupil who has severe and complex learning difficulties. Equipping pupils for independence extends well beyond their time in school. It is also about enriching their leisure time, enabling them to engage in social dialogue with their peers, for example. Significant numbers of pupils are now participating in chatrooms and discussion forums, with many of these being unregulated and even unmonitored. A project developed by the Scottish Sensory Centre (2001) as part of an online initiative to support families and children affected by visual impairment integrated a chatroom which is the UK's only safe and secure online environment for children with visual impairment. Some seventy-four children with visual impairment engaged in an online discussion forum, specifically designed to break down international barriers.

'Age-appropriateness' is an area worthy for consideration here. Indeed, we live in a society in which judgements by appearance are frequently promoted by the very technology we are trying to harness. The pupil who is seen as being different, or perhaps immature, in the activities he or she is undertaking, may provoke negative responses from peers despite the fact that the pupil is not only learning but also engaging with an activity independently. ICT can offer engagement with activities which not only meet specific learning difficulties but also package activities in ways that motivate the pupil in a context

---

Case study

John, a fourteen-year-old pupil with PMLD has been diagnosed with Fragile X, displays associated symptoms of attention deficits and over-activity and autistic-like features, such as hand flapping and poor eye contact. He finds watching the monitor or television screen disengaging and, whilst attracted by flashing colours and quick scene changes, is generally unable to focus on them for more than a few seconds. His class teacher has been focusing on developing John's visual tracking skills, using a series of switch-operated scenarios which deliver a range of sensory stimuli as animated objects and animals are activated. However, whilst John's responses became extended, his teacher investigated the use of more age-appropriate applications such as those provided by Priory Woods Special School. These freely download-able resources (available from http://www.priorywoods.middlesbrough.sch.uk/resources/restop.htm) include a collection of scenarios based on popular songs but set to animated figures which would not be out of place for a mainstream teenager's use. The quality of the presentations and their motivating impact on John promoted an engagement with the screen, particularly when they were then interfaced using an IWB.

However, John's teacher is starting to question the time spent on locating these resources, which tend to exhibit a limited 'shelf-life', and notes that John was actually more motivated by the use of his personal 'walkman' which allowed him to play cassettes of his favourite pieces of music – something he found more engaging and, indeed, more resilient to frequent use.

appropriate to his or her age group. Such factors need to be considered when devising a personalised, or differentiated, approach to learning which meets the specific needs identified.

There is always the possibility that ICT may not be as engaging for a pupil as we may have hoped or, indeed, the learning outcome is different to that planned. For some pupils with learning difficulties, particularly at the more complex end of the spectrum, 'concrete' scenarios may prove the best type of teaching resource. To be able to actually see and hold an object could prove far more stimulating than to see it represented on the screen. Indeed, it is the transparent nature of the technologies that can pose particular difficulties. Electronic 'distance' is an abstract concept and, consequently, can make outcomes using ICT difficult for the pupil with severe learning difficulties to connect with.

Activity

It is often presumed that the computer is a more effective learning tool than more traditional learning methods and resources. Teachers frequently spend very considerable lengths of time designing and creating specialised ICT-based activities designed to meet a pupil's very specific needs. Can you identify a scenario in which a pupil was engaged in an ICT-based activity in which the learning outcome was less successful than one which could have been provided by more traditional teaching methods?

The question remains, however, whether we as educators have been able to respond to the full potential that ICT offers pupils with SEN. Recent research indicated that some 92 per cent of teachers in the UK now consider themselves to be 'competent users' of ICT (e-Learning Foundation 2006), but it is essential that opportunities for professional development, as well as the time – and guidance – needed to develop skills which enable educators to identify and understand how very specific barriers to learning can be overcome through the application of ICT are given a high priority in all educational settings (Feldman 2003: 98). Equipping the educator for the rapidly evolving environment of change provides a real challenge for senior managers in schools.

It is certainly difficult to predict the future evolution of technology, but it is clear that with the implementation of high-speed connectivity, along with an innate desire by many educators to share not just ideas but also specialised curriculum resources will ensure that the Internet remains at the forefront as a tool for inclusion. Will this future, as the opening line of this chapter surmises, also include one in which the learning environment moves beyond the classroom in ways that start to break down the walls of the physical classroom? The DfES's Classroom of the Future project provides a glittering view of the classroom as a light and airy laboratory of learning and actually cites the inclusion of more pupils with SEN in mainstream schools (Teachernet 2006) as a key objective.

A competition organised by the *Guardian* newspaper in 2001 offered children the chance to express their own views on what their ideal school would look like. One striking comment, 'a school without walls so we can go outside to learn, with animals to look after and wild gardens to explore', is not as unrealistic as it seems. Whilst the role of the school within the community is currently being driven by an expansionist agenda (DfES 2006c), the increasingly imaginative use of VLEs can potentially, for example, blend school and home together. Most interestingly and particularly relevant to this chapter's theme, the Ultralab research unit at Anglia Polytechnic University has successfully run a pilot VLE, 'Notschool' (http://www.notschool.net), designed to re-engage pupils whose needs have been particularly challenging for schools to meet, including those who have been excluded, are disaffected, or are school-phobic.

It is clear that the new technologies have impressive credentials in the area of supporting learning and teaching for pupils with SEN. However, whilst we now have access to a tool previously unparalleled in terms of providing resources, its successful implementation must be, and always will be, dependent on the teacher's imagination, creativity and understanding of pupils' needs. Political agendas, target-setting processes and an ever-expanding curriculum must not impose barriers for educators to learn new skills and competencies in ICT.

7 Assessment and evaluation using ICT

Chapter overview

The QCA (2004) stipulates that progress in ICT must be reported as a separate subject as well as statements about learning across subjects. Judging and assessing the quality of achievement in ICT is set to become a central part of each child's school experience, and this chapter will describe and elucidate a number of ways of assessing and evaluating pupils' progress both in terms of their use of ICT across the curriculum and ICT as discrete subject provision. This chapter focuses on the following themes:

- the nature of assessment;
- the ways in which ICT knowledge, capabilities and skills are recorded;
- how the information gathered can be used to inform curriculum and lesson planning;
- the sorts of barriers to effective assessment that are highlighted in the research literature and ways of overcoming them;
- the monitoring and evaluation procedures used in schools and those recommended by research.

In this chapter, we will examine assessment within an ICT-based learning environment, assessment of learning of ICT knowledge and skills, and assessment of learning carried out with ICT as a useful aid. We begin with an exploration of the nature of assessment.

What is assessment?

Measuring children's progress seems to be a task teachers perform instinctively. Whether it is formalised in the guise of a written examination, continuous, as in project work, or informal, through a series of casual observations, assessment of learning remains one of the bedrock activities conducted on a daily basis in schools across the globe. There are many forms of assessment and many ways in which records of attainment can be gathered, stored and used.

Methods of assessment have often been scrutinised and challenged, but rarely are they revolutionised. However, due to recent advances in information technologies, assessment of learning is now undergoing change, leading to a critical reappraisal of the methods, rationale and processes of testing.

None would argue against assessment in schools, but we may question the emphasis placed upon assessment and the manner in which feedback is provided to learners (Fairbrother and Harrison 2001). In the light of innovation and change, teachers should also ask themselves: Is my method of assessment accurate, or effective, or even relevant?

Am I measuring what I think I am measuring, and is my method of assessment fair to all my students?

Activity

Think back to your own school experiences. What were the worst aspects of assessment and testing for you? What were the best aspects?

With the growth of opportunities to use ICT in the classroom, new learning activities are constantly being devised, so it follows that new methods of assessment might also be developed or adapted to measure learning within these new contexts.

Many different and often opposing theories underlie, shape and inform the various methods of assessment currently in use in schools, but it can be a difficult task to determine which theory is the most accurate in representing the reality of classroom learning. For example, can teachers ensure that the method of assessment they are using is the most effective, or is it doing 'more harm than good'? Do certain assessment methods alienate children, or demotivate them? Ultimately, teachers should ask: Why do we assess at all?

Activity

Spend a few minutes listing some reasons why assessment of children's learning is necessary.

Assessment of children's learning is necessary for at least six key reasons:

1 Feedback
2 Monitoring progress
3 Informing parents
4 Evaluation
5 Research
6 Legal requirements.

First, if managed effectively, formalised assessment should provide the learner with clear feedback on performance. It provides students with the opportunity to discover their weak and strong points in any given subject domain or skill area. Effective feedback from an experienced teacher is clearly a particularly important component in the academic development process for all children, regardless of their age or ability. Constructive and supportive feedback also motivates children to raise their levels of skill and understanding, so this aspect of assessment can provide much-needed impetus.

Second, assessment should contribute towards the maintenance of records of a student's progress over a period of time. Measuring achievement over time enables teachers to monitor improvement and provide important intervention if and when children require it so they are kept on target.

Third, parents and guardians require information about their children's learning. Parents and guardians have a right to be kept informed as important stakeholders in the schooling of their child. Assessment provides clear indicators of achievement for them and facilitates constructive dialogue between carer and teacher.

Fourth, assessment can feed into the curriculum-evaluation process. Teachers need to know how effective a course, scheme of work or lesson plan can be in meeting the educational needs of the child, as well as monitoring the extent to which it meets the expectations of the school, education authority and funding bodies. Teachers also need to know to what extent their teaching methods and resources are helping learners to achieve learning outcomes. Assessment statistics can, thus, be applied as quality indicators.

Fifth, assessment can also contribute towards a better appreciation of learning processes and can help teachers to understand what works best in the classroom and why that is the case. Forms of action research, based on reflection of professional practice, can be informed by and through the assessment of learning. Teachers should continually revise and refine assessment strategies as a result of their own reflective observations (Argyris and Schön 1974) to more closely measure student learning against the learning outcomes they have formulated (Clarke 2005).

Finally, assessment is, of course, a legal requirement. Funding bodies require information to show how successfully schools deliver a curriculum, and standard attainment tests provide them with this information.

We could also discuss the role assessment plays in motivating students to engage with learning and encouraging them to achieve. Formative modes of assessment, for example, enable children to visualise their goals and encourage them to aim for targets. Countering this, of course, are the negative connotations of assessment, including the problems it creates for students should they fail, or the issues that emerge when assessment is ineffective.

Later in this chapter, we will examine some of the ways in which effective assessment can be applied within an ICT learning context, and we will also explore how ICT can be used as an assessment tool in its own right. Before this, we offer a survey of some of the approaches to assessment commonly seen in schools, along with a few of the less familiar modes.

Modes of assessment

Diagnostic assessment

This kind of assessment is generally performed when students first arrive in a new classroom. The experienced teacher will apply this form of assessment instinctively and usually informally. At one level, diagnostic assessment can be used to indicate deficits in skills or knowledge, whilst at another level it can be used to flag up difficulties a child may be experiencing, such as indicators of cognitive impairment, dyslexia or other special needs. In Chapter 6 we provide an in-depth examination of SEN and the use of ICT as an enabling resource.

Formative assessment

Generally, this kind of measurement is informal and often discreet. Formative assessment can be conducted through observation, questioning or testing. It provides the teacher with indicators of how well each student is coping with the subject matter and to what extent they are achieving their targets. As was indicated earlier, it can also be used to provide students with goals to achieve and targets to aim for.

Summative assessment

There is a variety of summative assessment types, including written tests, coursework and, in the case of languages, oral examinations. Fairbrother and Harrison (2001) believe that there are three ways of gaining information from students: namely, written, oral and practical. Essentially, all achieve the same purpose – they provide teachers with clear indicators of the attainment levels of each student within a given subject and are usually measured in a norm-referenced format. Computer-based forms of summative assessment (sometimes referred to as computer-aided assessment or CAA) are already used in further and higher education. Due to restrictions in the software, questions are commonly presented as multiple choice or multiple response. This has generated debate over the depth of knowledge and understanding CAA can measure. This is an issue teachers need to address – CAA is beginning to appear in primary and secondary education and will be discussed later in this chapter.

Norm-referenced assessment

The concept of norm-referencing assessment stems from a perception that all learners can be measured against a 'normal' level of achievement associated with a specific age range. This belief derives from stage theories of learning such as the cognitive maturation model proposed by developmental psychologist Jean Piaget. Pupils who score low in attainment tests are assumed to be 'below' the expected level of attainment, whilst those who score higher than the expected average are assumed to be high achievers.

Criterion-referenced assessment

For many teachers, criterion-referenced assessment is accepted as a much fairer system. All students are judged according to the same assessment criteria, so, in principle, if all perform to the same standard, all should receive the same grade (Fairbrother and Harrison, 2001). Therefore, if a test is delivered through some form of CAA, in the form of multiple-choice questions, each student should have exactly the same chance to score high marks providing their knowledge is adequate. Computer-based testing of this kind will eliminate all subjectivity. This form of objective testing is fair but, as has already been indicated, can at the same time be superficial, as it often tests simple recall of factual information rather than deeper knowledge or cognitive skills.

Self-assessment

This is where students are encouraged to report on their own levels of attainment. Potentially, ICT can provide a very powerful tool for this kind of assessment. Fox (2003) offers a number of self-assessment ICT-based activities, such as each child maintaining a personal record of ICT-based learning through the construction of a folder of printouts. Other physical evidence of ICT expertise might include an organised collection of digital images or listings of web addresses. Students could also harness the power of the web to develop records of their personal achievements, including the creation of web-logs and personal home pages. Children have a natural tendency to measure themselves against their peers, which, on an informal basis, can be a double-edged sword, as it can either foster competition and motivate or negatively affect self-esteem and demotivate. Either way, this kind of norm-referenced assessment must be approached cautiously and would normally be inappropriate as a formal assessment method. However, there are many useful informal approaches to self-assessment that use digital resources. Later in this chapter, some useful examples are presented.

Peer assessment

Children can, and often do, assess each other's work. Research from more than thirty years ago suggests that children as young as eight years old have the ability to assess each other's work accurately and fairly (Nash 1973). Yet, peer assessment should be adopted with caution, as children's forthright comments can sometimes be detrimental to the recipient's self-esteem. Encouraging children to fairly assess each other's work and to accept constructive criticism are life skills that should be nurtured, as the earlier in life they are acquired, the better prepared the child will be to enter the world of work.

Triadic assessment

This form of assessment involves input from teacher, student and peers. It is used most extensively in adult-education contexts, but there are opportunities for teachers to employ it effectively in any sector of education. Providing the above measures are cautiously applied, and processes are closely monitored, triadic assessment should yield valuable results for all those involved. Creating a digital record of this kind of three-way appraisal of achievement can provide parents and teachers alike with clear indicators of the child's progress. The records can then be easily updated, corrected, stored, retrieved and shared to all stakeholders in a common format.

Ipsative assessment

This is a little-known concept for many teachers, and it relates to the assessment of a child against his or her own previous achievements. Ipsative assessment is most commonly used within SEN contexts, and, although probably the fairest method of assessment available, it is time-intensive, highly personalised and, if used in mainstream contexts, would be unacceptable to most examining bodies or inspection teams. On an informal basis, however, teachers could employ this approach in the assessment of students' production of ICT-based artefacts. Over time, for example, children develop their skills in the application of programmable technologies such as roamers and pixies, and these skills can enhance their knowledge of geometric shapes and mathematical calculation, so measuring personal progress over time could prove effective in a cross-curricular context.

Activity

Which of the above methods of assessment have you used or seen used in your own professional practice?

Which do you consider to be the least and most problematic in your own subject speciality? What reasons can you offer?

Barriers to effective assessment

There are many aspects of assessment that create problems for schools or cause consternation amongst teachers. Some are practically related to issues such as resourcing or time, whilst others are more theoretical in nature. Some forms of assessment also cause distress for pupils, particularly if they are placed in lower streams because of poor examination results.

Activity

What do you consider to be the greatest barriers to effective assessment?

All teachers have stories to tell about assessment. Much research has also been undertaken in the area, and a combination of anecdotal and empirical evidence is useful in highlighting some of the key issues.

Reliability

One difficulty to overcome in assessment is the issue of *reliability*. If a test or exam does not hold its consistency across many students, groups, years and assessors, then it is probably unreliable. Reliable forms of assessment should provide similar feedback when testing students who are at a similar attainment level. Lack of reliability in assessment results would leave teachers unsure how well results of testing reflected the ability and knowledge levels of each learner. One of the tasks of software developers is to create software that can assist and support this process.

Validity

Another challenging area is whether or not assessment has *validity* – that is, whether it measures the stated aims and outcomes of a lesson or whether a child's performance is accurately being measured. Cotton (1995) proposes four key types of assessment validity.

First, assessment must be seen by students to be relevant. This kind of validity addresses the expectations of the learner. Examining them at a level or subject matter above or below their current knowledge level would be irrelevant and would be seen to lack *face validity*.

Second, assessment cannot be exclusive. All learners must have an equal chance to succeed in their learning and should all be measured equitably, as without this 'level playing field', assessment would lack *empirical validity*.

Third, if students are judged on a particular skill, performance or knowledge base in a manner that is inappropriate, the assessment would lack *construct validity*. Assessing a learner's ability in speaking and listening through the use of a written test, for example, would be an unsuitable method.

Finally, teachers should know how to identify learner attributes that are the most important to assess within a given knowledge or skill domain. Doing so is sometimes quite difficult, but to succeed would ensure that the method of assessment had *concurrent validity*.

Together, these types of validity ensure that students are assessed fairly, relevantly and accurately, to provide a picture of their current skills and knowledge range and an indication of their deficits so that targets can be created to encourage progress.

Record-keeping

Poor record-keeping is a barrier to effective assessment. Teachers who fail to track student progress through accurate, comprehensive records are in danger of missing key information about learners' progress. With easy-to-use databases and spreadsheets, teachers should be able to maintain up-to-date and comprehensive records which are quickly accessible and directly transferable to other storage media, for example, management-information systems or high-density data drives. One of the most useful attributes of ICT is the user's capability to create, store, share and retrieve information in a universally compatible format. Wireless and Bluetooth applications are the latest in a long line of computer-based solutions that facilitate easier sharing and distribution of digital information between professionals. Record-keeping has never been simpler, because ICT offers teachers access to important information on each child's academic progress.

Assessing learning within an ICT context

To be effective as assessors, teachers need to be familiar with a number of assessment strategies and should also apprise themselves of the benefits and limitations of each. Assessing learning within the subject of ICT can be problematic, due to the complex interplay between fine motor skills (keyboard, mouse), learning and cognition. On the other hand, learning assessment in general has become more accessible in the digital age. The use of ICT as a tool for assessment is beginning to yield dividends, with many software applications already being used regularly in classrooms.

Using diagnostic software to test for learning deficits is recommended, as is hybrid software that provides a number of key functions such as assessment of learning within specific core subject areas and the generation of individual learning plans.

To be effective ICT learning assessors, teachers also need to be very familiar with a wide range of software skills. Many teachers lack confidence in this area and feel threatened by the idea of assessing ICT skills in children who may be more adept than they are (NGfL2006). As a result of these skills deficiencies, or in some cases the teacher's self-perception of skills deficiency, there have been discrepancies in assessment of ICT learning from school to school. It is doubly important then that teachers not only acquire more advanced skills and knowledge *about* ICT but also that they also become more familiar with how these can be assessed *through* the use of ICT.

Using ICT as an assessment tool

Earlier in this chapter, we argued that ICT can be extremely useful and effective as an assessment tool, and there is one notable instance of successful use reported in the literature.

Examples of computer-based record-keeping

Hicks and Bishop (2005) document the use of an online assessment tool in their account 'Schools without Walls'. The online resource, located at http://www.online-assessments. co.uk provides each primary-school pupil with an individual learning plan and offers teachers clear indicators of each child's learning gains within each specific core-curriculum subject.

Earlier, we alluded to the idea that self-assessment of learning can be a useful and relevant activity for informal testing. Where the acquisition of ICT skills is of interest, there are several useful tools. The example below (Figure 7.1), developed by St Helens Council, provides Key Stage 1 children with a template to measure their progress. These columns are worded to indicate that the child can perform 'with help', 'on my own', and that s/he can 'show someone else', and to reflect increasing expertise in each developing skill. Children can demonstrate these skill levels to a teacher or classroom worker and then tick off each box, demonstrating their increasing competencies whilst engendering a growing sense of achievement and pride in their learning. As an added incentive, each of the discrete skills has an illustration attached.

An integrated task is included at the foot of each task list, requiring the learner to use all of the preceding skills to complete successfully. The assessment sheet is completed by a useful section in which the child tells what they enjoyed and what they think they could have done a little better. Each form is signed by the pupil and the teacher, sealing a useful partnership in ICT skills assessment.

Objective: To use a word bank and word processing program on my own. To write sentences. To know that my writing can be changed, printed and shared with others.		With help	On my own	Show someone else
I used:				
	Type my own words, delete mistakes with the backspace key and then print			
	Make the computer say a sound			
	Choose words from a word bank to make my own sentence			
	Find the main keys on the keyboard			
	Begin to use the mouse to make changes or add words			
	Make changes to my work and explain how I made the changes			
	Integrated Task: Do a piece of writing about............................ .... And print it			
I enjoyed:				
What I could have done better:				

Figure 7.1 Assessment sheet.
Source: St Helen's Council learning zone: primary self-assessment Key Stage 1.

Another useful digital ICT recording system is that offered by Wokingham Local Education Authority (see Figure 7.2). Created by help2learn, this is a more formalised recording sheet, and based in Excel, but with the same three attainment levels for pupils to tick electronically.

These examples are useful to distinguish the differences between pupil oriented assessment tools that are ICT supported (Figure 7.1) and tools that are electronically managed (Figure 7.2).

Chapter summary

We have seen that there are many reasons why assessment is conducted in schools. We also explored several of the assessment methods that are available and examined the strengths and limitations of each. We identified several barriers to effective assessment, including lack of reliability, lack of validity and poor record-keeping – the latter being a problem that is most easily addressed through the use of appropriate computer software.

Record-keeping has never been easier, since the introduction of easy-to-use spreadsheets and databases. These offer teachers the electronic means to create, update, store, retrieve and share important information on a child's academic progress. Relational databases offer the user the ability to cross-reference, search for specific categories and generate reports on specific queries from the database. We suggest that teachers who are engaged in teaching ICT should familiarise themselves with some of the growing number of computer-based record-keeping methods that are available.

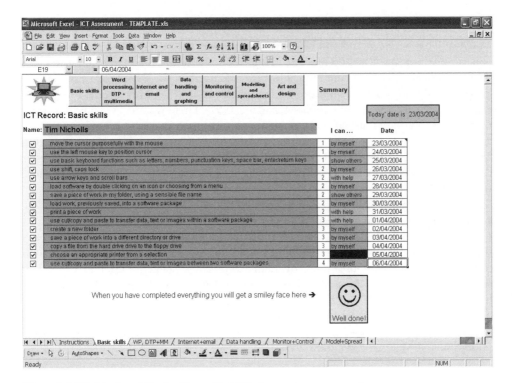

Figure 7.2 Wokingham District Council's ICT electronic assessment form.
Source: Created by Tim Nicholls (http://help2learn.co.uk>).

8 New technologies and the curriculum

Chapter overview

It is possible that the uneasy tensions between teachers and technology can subsume more fundamental issues where ICT is used in school settings. One of the marginal constituencies within the digital classroom is where ICT is directly brought to bear as a support for curriculum delivery. In this chapter, we explore some of the key issues where technology and curriculum are juxtaposed, to enable you to:

*   understand the importance of subjects when developing cross-curricular strategies;
*   appreciate the complexities of relating digital technologies across the curriculum;
*   evaluate some practical uses of ICTs in various subject areas.

Introduction

Much of what has been said and written about new technologies has focused mainly on generic teaching and learning processes. As a result, the research literature indicates that levels of collaboration and communication are enhanced by the skilled use of ICT, as are knowledge-building and thinking skills (Sandholtz *et al.* 1996, Howe *et al.* 1996, Light *et al.* 1996, Knight and Knight 1995, McFarlane 1997). There is some evidence, however, that new technologies also afford a range of opportunities that can transform teaching and offer improved possibilities for subject and disciplinary learning (Vaughn 1997, Barton 1997, Haydn 2003, John 2005, Ruthven *et al.* 2005). In essence, new technologies can offer different advantages to a range of different subjects both in primary and secondary school (Haydn 2003).

A central proposition underpinning much of the research in this area is that teaching and learning are often linked to the cultures of subjects. Our use of the term 'subject sub-culture', therefore, relies on the definition offered by Goodson (1993, 1997). He argues that subjects are well-established bodies of knowledge and social practices that carry with them particular assumptions about 'worthwhile knowledge', 'effective teaching', 'the good student' and 'appropriate assessment'. The traditions that give rise to these sub-cultures are, however, more complex and tend to be rooted in school and organisational structures, collective experience and, more recently, the National Curriculum directives. They are also sites where teachers are able to express their own personal theories and pedagogical styles (Goodson and Mangan 1995, John 2005).

Subjects, the curriculum and new technologies

Much of the debate around the educational value and purpose of ICT has been set within a 'cultures in tension' thesis which tries to explain the resistance of accepted subject sub-cultures to the incorporation of ICT into their curricular and pedagogic processes. These conflicting rationales have led to a number of explanations including subject resistance (Finlayson and Perry 1995), technophobia (Selwyn *et al.* 2001) and 'technological colonisation' (Goodson and Mangan 1995: 626). Questions arise as to whether ICT should be taught as a discrete subject or as embedded within all other subjects across the curriculum. As a result, the teaching of ICT (rather than teaching with or via ICT) has meant that, as Barnett (1994: 62), puts it:

> an arrangement by which responsibility for practical capability rested with technology and for critical awareness with subjects such as social studies, history or religious education, that is, where values had been driven into exile from out of technology, would be undesirable. This would tend to confirm technology as a ghetto for ingenious tinkerers, and the humanities as the natural home for anti-technologists.

Indeed, as Watson (2001) points out, not only are the vocational aspects dominant, they are also narrowly technocentric. However, recent National Curriculum pronouncements have tried to create a rapprochement between subject areas and new technology (DfEE 2000). Teachers and students are now being exhorted to use ICT tools and information sources to support their work in subjects – giving ICT tools new pedagogical purpose (OfSTED 2001). Reconciling the two has proved problematic, however. The core of the problem resides in the basic units of organisation around which secondary-school curricula are built. The dominance of the subject department combined with the rapid socialisation into a subject sub-culture (Lacey 1977, Goodson and Marsh, 1998) has created a set of lenses through which national and school policy are filtered.

The centrality of subject culture and its relationship to the classroom uses of ICT also conforms to other themes in the literature about ICT use. Andrews (2000: 26), for instance, claims that the 'humanities based, liberal and book-dominated culture of English . . . is undoubtedly a factor in the resistance of English teachers to new technologies'. John and LaVelle (2004) similarly point out that the more overtly empirical disciplines such as mathematics and science have a greater affinity with technology, while the humanities and music are more sceptical. Loveless and Ellis (2001) also highlight the importance of subject epistemologies and related pedagogical beliefs and their effects on technological integration.

In terms of ICT deployment and use, some subjects have been seen as barriers both to effective integration and transformation of practice. In a study of subject sub-culture, teaching style and levels of integration of ICT, Goodson and Mangan (1995) found that humanities and arts-based teachers were often reluctant users of new technology when it was perceived to be at odds with the norms of their subject. The authors also highlighted the tension between technology-favouring subjects and those whose teachers felt their core values were fundamentally at variance with ICT (Wheeler and Winter 2005). The latter feared colonisation and the replacement of academic learning with the technological; in such cases, the computer was tolerated and co-opted, becoming one tool amongst many. Selwyn (1999), in his study of the influence of subject cultures on differentiated computer use, found that both students and teachers constructed their 'computer identities' in terms of their subject courses and that these identities were shaped by a variety of personal predilections. He explained how, when faced with a perceived threat to the norms and traditions of their subject, some teachers retreat quickly into their subject sub-culture.

Selwyn (1999) explains this process using Lave and Wenger's (1991) and Wenger's (1990) notion of cultural transparency. He argues that for ICT to be used successfully in a subject area, its significance as a learning tool must be highly visible, while at the same time, its role as a mediating technology supporting the visibility of the subject matter must render it invisible. The balance between the two therefore becomes crucial if ICT is to play a significant role in both developing and transforming subject pedagogy and learning. However, Selwyn (1999) found that in ICT-resistant subject communities, the role of transparency is reversed. Then, computers become highly visible as mediating technologies (often getting in the way of learning) and highly invisible as learning tools (either hidden away or given limited prominence) within the subject arena. Other studies (Ruthven *et al.* 2004, Bishop 1998) claim that school subjects, their pedagogical discourses and related practices shape ICT use, making it visible and giving force to learning. They also highlight the importance of pupil agency in this learning process.

Activity

Can you think of any other issues that might hinder or encourage the use of new technology when planning and teaching subject content? How has technology been incorporated into classrooms and subject areas?

Research sample and methodology

The participants were thirty-seven secondary-school subject teachers who had been involved with the InterActive Education Project at various levels for four years. The teachers were interviewed as part of the final evaluation of the InterActive Project and were drawn from across the disciplines. Although the sample was not categorised specifically by age and experience, all participants had between three and seventeen years experience of classroom teaching. Those being interviewed included: mathematics ($n = 9$), science ($n = 7$), English ($n = 8$), modern foreign languages ($n = 6$), music ($n = 4$), geography ($n = 3$). All taught across Key Stages 3 and 4.

The participants were interviewed after the conclusion of the project and were questioned about their involvement in the project. The questions included a mixture of descriptive, process and evaluative types, the purpose being to ascertain the teachers' perceptions of the relative successes, problems and challenges of working with ICT in different subject areas. The interviews were semi-structured and lasted between one hour and one hour and forty-five minutes. Each interview was audio-taped and then transcribed for analysis.

In order to create category codes for the data sets, Strauss and Corbin's (1990) constant comparative method was used. The analysis was, therefore, defined by a set of connected stages. In Stage 1 the transcripts were read a number of times in order to identify strong themes and the relationships between them. In Stage 2 the emerging themes were turned into succinct category codes. The corpus of interview data was then subjected to a thematic analysis based on these categories. The categories were also given strong support-ing descriptions in order to improve the reliability of the coding process. Each category was described in detail, thus forming the basis to the coding scheme.

At Stage 3, the transcripts were read and re-read in order to create 'sentence units' using the category descriptions; the 'sentence units' were shaped using both single-word or term labels (for instance, practice, teaching, learning, teaching style, subject, content, subject matter, etc.), and short category-implying phrases, for example, 'focus more on the process of teaching and on the process of learning'. A total of 1,850 parsed sentence units were identified.

At Stage 4, the initial coding was then checked for reliability by two independent 'experts' to adjudicate using 10 per cent of the transcripts. High inter-coder reliability coefficients of 0.72 and 0.89 were obtained using the Scott formula (Ober *et al.* 1971). The first-level analysis sought to reduce the regularity of the 'sentence units' to percentages of the total within the six-category framework. The second level proceeded to use the category labels to highlight the percentage of regularity of comment according to subject area. The 'sentence units' formed the basis to a more fine-grained qualitative exemplar-based account of the data.

Findings

Engagement or enablement?

Most respondents were generally supportive of the use of ICT in their subject areas and had a realistic view of its potential to enhance teaching and learning. The idea that ICT has the capacity to create potent learning opportunities across the curriculum in a way that might empower students and create more individualised learning was seen as powerful. This view was consistent with many of their espoused theories about what constituted good practice in their subject areas and their conceptions of the ideal student. For some, ICT articulated strongly with their belief that new technology might provide greater opportunities for experimentation in the classroom and thereby change radically the relationship between teacher, learner and subject. The following extract from a mathematics teacher was typical:

Q: How might ICT change practice?
T: I think ICT has the possibility to really change things in classrooms if it is used thoughtfully. At the moment we are only skirting around the edges and we need to take some risks. I know well this might not be popular but if we don't then we might just go through the motions and then it will become boring like any other resource. We need to be bold – experiment a bit – then it might begin to really take off and start to change practice.
Q: For the better?
T: I think so . . . it might bring back some old ideas in a new form, sort of getting away from telling and more . . . working with ideas and questions, quite liberating I suppose.

Much of this connection between personal theories and the enabling potential of ICT was underpinned by a 'powerful apparatus' idea of new technology. Here a small number of interviewees claimed that ICT was more than a 'useful extra' in the classroom and had the ability to move beyond 'shaping and styling', allowing the products produced by students to challenge the nature of knowledge. This expressed position was in marked contrast to the majority of teachers who saw ICT as a 'polishing tool', which provided students with the possibility of revising the text to improve both its style and substance. This view was tied into the potential of ICT to personalise knowledge as well as represent its plurality. Such perceptions were particularly marked amongst the English teachers.

The idea of ICT as a 'polishing tool' ran parallel to a series of thoughts that cohere under the category 'informational uses'. Many saw new technologies as providing an expanding base of accessible information that could be accessed rapidly and accurately by students. The variety of interactive technology, whether the Internet, CD-ROM or DVD, also enthused teachers. Some saw the possibilities for creative collaboration between students and between themselves and students; others saw the potential for changing the nature of the classroom and its traditional format. A few gave forthright examples of how such change might proceed. An English teacher explained that she could already see her students 'moving around the classroom gathering knowledge from the net, video, CDs and books then storing it and maybe even interrogating it' before moving to 'publish either as a web page, or a PowerPoint presentation or whatever'. Such a view was rare in the transcripts, although others offered similar but less well-developed scenarios. All pointed to the power of new information outlets to help students understand the subject while simultaneously developing new forms of 'information literacy', and in this regard the English teachers evinced a more evangelical position. Finally, some pointed to the importance of this knowledge base in ending the traditional elision between home and school.

Much of the enthusiasm for such new pedagogic moves also came from each teachers' own uses of technology. All, to a greater or lesser extent, used the Internet and other technological databases at home, and as a result they felt confident in using the technology as well as being familiar with interfaces and formats. This tacit confidence clearly spilled over into their professional lives proving, at least at the level of espoused theory, that when competence and confidence are high, then enthusiasm for ICT improves. The most widespread professional use related to lesson-planning and the production of resources (Counsell 2003). All recognised the power of ICT to create high-quality classroom resources in minimal time. This was accentuated by the use of search engines, websites, interactive multimedia and word-processing. Additionally, many used ICT to carry out basic administration including record-keeping, assessment and the storage of data. A number also pointed to 'home use' as being important, and here the crossover with professional uses became apparent. One commented:

> I use it for booking holidays, pricing things, e-mail and just general interest. Sometimes I use the net to look up ideas of teaching and I get on the subject sites. Some are better than others, but it's useful. I use Word for word-processing and PowerPoint . . . oh yes I use Excel for my household bills and things. It's handy using them because then you can do the same in school . . . you know their capabilities – what they should be used for and when.

Friend or foe?

The subject area (Goodson and Mangan 1995) also provided an important foundation upon which most teachers in the sample based many of their epistemological, pedagogical and personal theories. However, the data revealed a number of subtle discordances when it came to the challenge of ICT. Science, for instance, has a long association with new technologies, and as a discipline was responsible for many of the changes in policy and practice that were brought about by, for example, the liberating effect of computing power. This close relationship continued into the educational field as science was one of the first school subjects to integrate technology successfully into its curriculum. An example of this effect in science might be the liberation to higher-order skills of science process by data logging (Baggott la Velle *et al.* 2003a). Other science teachers in our sample felt that ICT should only be used when it has an explicitly positive effect on pupils' performance in the curriculum, and here there was an implicit assumption of the measurement of this performance against the specific assessment instruments of the UK's National Curriculum (Baggott la Velle *et al.* 2003b). Many interviewees also stressed the importance of simulation as the one tool that might be powerful in offering students a sense of what Latour (1999) calls 'realistic realism'.

In music and English, there had been less contact with ICT, and this was reflected in the responses, despite the fact that the popular music revolution relied on the integration and innovative use of new technologies such as Musical Instrument Digital Interface (MIDI). In classrooms, the impact had been far less significant; nevertheless, the music teachers interviewed were very positive about the potential. For them, it represented a way of integrating performance with composition as well as challenging the performative nature of the subject. For some, it was also a 'democratising tool' in that it allowed children with little traditional cultural capital to express their musicality with devices that connected with their personal experience of music. Finally, ICT was perceived as giving music the opportunity to 'update itself' and move away from the standard instrument image.

In English, ICT has been seen as a potential challenge to the humanities, liberal, literature-dominated culture of the subject that has been pervasive in many departments. Goodwyn (1997) claims that this is still one of the main factors militating against the rapid take-up of new technologies within the subject. Conversely, there is also a tradition of seeing English as offering students the opportunity to explore personal meanings through language and other expressive forms, and here the blending of ICT with media studies is, according to Goodwyn (2000), leading to a new 'rhetoric of the arts'. These positions were visible in the interviews, with most focusing on the possibilities inherent in the technologies. Finally, in history, the penetration of ICT has been patchy despite a number of initiatives. During recent years with the support of HABET – the Historical Association's advisory body on educational technology – and the pioneering work of many individuals (Haydn 2003, Counsell 2003), ICT has made some inroads into the subject. However, in many respects, historians have, perhaps, been the most resistant to technology, often falling back on the essential humanism at the core of the subject. This was reflected in the interviews, although, for many, the technology was not the issue but rather it was the way it was being used to represent the subject that raised concerns. One interviewee opined:

> History is sometimes forgotten in all the hoo-ha about ICT. I don't see the point of using it if it doesn't add to the subject, to the learning process involved. I feel that it's [seen as] an add-on something that will automatically improve understanding in the subject – this is simply not true and needs to be nailed.

The teachers in the sample also saw the location and dispersal of hardware as a challenge. Here concerns tended to cross subject boundaries as more generic issues came to the fore. Some feared that the leaving of an established subject base with its recognisable features was potentially disruptive and preferred using mobile sets of laptops rather than move to the computer room. Others felt that the lure of the screen might pose fewer problems but added that in any computer lesson, 'planning has to be more precise, and the tasks have to be very specific, otherwise the lesson will run away from you very quickly'. Such a comment was typical and reinforces the notion that unless carefully structured, ICT can quickly turn a lesson into a series of unstructured off-task activities. Many were also concerned about the lack of opportunity in computer rooms for whole-class teaching.

Content and pedagogy

Two prominent categories in the data referred to the ways in which the subject-specific pedagogy related to the use of ICT. Many of the respondents raised the issue of the relationship between what they regarded as 'subject pedagogy' and the underlying assumptions of ICT. Although suspicious at first about the 'techno' agenda, the majority of the interviewees admitted that over time the distinction between their teaching styles and the use of ICT tended to diminish, and that by the end of their involvement with the InterActive Project, they had begun to notice fewer differences between how they taught, the subject content and the use of the technology. Comments included:

> The overlap with what might be termed 'traditional' language work is excellent and it just offers other ways of approaching the subject that are genuine means of teaching and more importantly they don't interfere with how I teach, they seem to work with it.
>
> (Modern foreign languages – MFL 6)

> The art of it is choosing the moment and then seeing the opportunities to develop the ideas in a new style of teaching that blends with my usual practice and the topics that I'm working on in Geography.
>
> (Geography – GEO 3)

> So they [the students] seemed to see the connections more clearly because of hyperlinks. This makes the teaching more powerful because the properties of the technology reinforce a way of teaching we use. It also helps to consolidate the subject learning through the teaching – that's why I tend not to notice any difference now between what the computer can do and what I do.
>
> (English – ENG 7)

Activity

What do the comments from the three teachers suggest about the ways in which new technologies should be used when planning for teaching?

These comments reflect a wide range of responses that indicate the ways in which extended use under supportive conditions helps to blend ICT with subject-specific pedagogy. According to the interview responses, this blending works in a number of different ways: in one sense, it acts as a lever helping teachers make their recognisable practice more effective; in another, it acts as a fulcrum by facilitating degrees of reorientation – and possible transformation – within that practice (Kerr 1991, Ruthven *et al.* 2003). However, of importance was the fact that for the pedagogy to blend and for the ICT to have any learning effect, then the subject content had to have resonance with the technology, while the pedagogy used must be seen to 'fit' with the learning outcomes (both tacit and explicit) designated by the teacher.

It also became clear that many of the physical barriers to ICT use needed to be overcome before the blend could be operationalised. These barriers included:

- the inflexibility of the curriculum;
- the 'out-dated' structure of many schemes of work;
- the 'stiff' and 'pencil and paper'-driven assessment structures;
- the lack of 'laptops';
- the 'unfriendliness', the 'cold', the 'techie', the 'awkward', the 'neutral' computer labs;
- the lack of appropriate and regular 'on tap' technical support.

Prominent among these was the dislike of the 'computer room', where many felt that the subject became decontextualised and where the teaching and learning styles became dictated by the location. For many, the computer room represented the vocational curriculum made manifest; it was seen as the place where highly prescribed activities are introduced and practised in routine situations. These more esoteric concerns were matched by more direct professional challenges. The 'technologised' room, many feared, might lead to an instant loss of face if competence and confidence were perceived to be low. In English, geography and modern foreign languages, the use of laptops seemed to offer the potential for greater permeability between the perceived functional discourse underlying ICT and the more liberal humanistic discourse underpinning their subject. However, it was felt that this permeability would only continue if schools, policy-makers and professional development providers recognised the validity of both discourses and began to resource schools accordingly (Watson 2001). As teachers put it:

> This 'computer room' is more than a room for the machines, it is about technology and about preparing kids for work. I hate it – it's so cold and unfriendly, it represents the geeky side of computers and it can be frightening.
>
> (Geography – GEO 3)

> Schools have got to get their heads around this idea of teaching and stop buying kit all the time. They always seem to have new computer rooms and I just don't buy this ICT as a subject stuff . . . reeks of the factory and factory fodder . . . I'm about making children think through maths.
>
> (Maths – MA 4)

> I have really benefited from using the new simulations and so have the kids – they have really engaged with it and I think their learning has come on in leaps and bounds – but we must make sure that schools and heads don't think this is a simple and cheap answer – we need lab resources desperately and books and equipment not more computer rooms which tend to limit teaching. These are not opposites, they should really be part of the same process – education, I think it's called.
>
> (Science – SCI 8)

Activity

Do you agree with the comments that computer labs/rooms are difficult to teach in? What balance should there be between real and virtual teaching resources?

Congruence and learning

Selwyn (1999), Counsell (2003) and Ruthven *et al.* (2004) all point to the need for high levels of congruence between the technology and the subject if ICT use is to become more widespread and effective in schools. This relates to Counsell's (2004) idea of Type A and Type B resource. Here, an ICT resource of the Type A variety means that the learning focus is intrinsic to the ICT use; in other words, the technology enhances the learning in ways that would not be possible without it. A Type B resource, on the other hand, has a lower convergence with the learning activity and is more of an added extra. In the data, the higher the convergence of the ICT resource with the subject focus and the planned learning outcomes, the more likely it was that extended use would occur. Furthermore, it was here that new technologies appear to have most transformative potential by helping learners acquire new knowledge and understanding, deploy critical thinking skills and develop new forms of creativity (Noss and Pachler 1999). The following comments are offered in support of the distinction:

> The focus on the data in the second SDI [single document interface] and the way it was integrated more fully when I was planning the lessons helped them to develop supported conclusions about their area and they had better in depth conclusions and better evaluations than previously. It was like a jigsaw fitting together.
>
> (English – ENG 6)

> Their learning seemed to be more genuine the second time around, and it made me realise that I was making proper use of ICT – but it was all in planning really. The schemes of work were flexible enough, and I was able to see how the digital cameras and Excel could fit with my aims and objectives for the lessons and the fieldwork.
>
> (Geography – GEO 1)

> It's easy to just plonk them in front of a screen or just get them to do things with Word – drop-downs, word searches, you know that sort of stuff – but to really get them thinking about using drop-downs to improve their vocab and their thinking in French means you have to plan it carefully so it links with your aims and with how you work with the kids.
>
> (Modern foreign languages – MFL 2)

> What using ICT did do was help me focus more on the process of teaching and on the process of learning than I would usually have done. I suppose it was because it forced me to think about how I teach, and the mental awareness that came along with it was the most beneficial factor. I also began to realise that my teaching style was changing – bit by bit – and that the software – the Sketchpad – was just . . . part of the furniture.
>
> (Maths – MA 8)

Activity

What do these comments suggest about the relationship between lesson planning, new technology and the curriculum?

We used PowerPoint a lot and e-mail and the web – you know, for resources and images – but when you put them together you realise that you couldn't do the multi-modal stuff without the technology. It's the technology that allows you to teach – that's been an eye-opener.

(English – ENG 5)

Three years ago, I couldn't compare regions – well, I could, but it was slow – but now we can get instant comparisons and analyses from outside the UK as well. That means the fieldwork is changing; the whole geography thing is changing; ICT is – I know this might sound daft – but it's kind of changing the subject and me along with it.

(Geography – GEO 2)

Modern foreign languages and English teachers felt that the recognisability of the interfaces combined with their functionality seemed to free teachers and students from making a distinction between the technology and the subject. It is important to qualify these comments with the fact that these teachers tended to use generic software rather than subject-specific applications that were more prevalent in science and mathematics.

So it can be the same with vocab and you can target key grammatical concepts as well. So the overlap with what might be termed 'traditional' language work is excellent, and it just offers another way of approaching the subject that is genuine. Some were even beginning to think about audience and how a different language and a style had to be adopted. The beauty of technology is that they can do this from within the draft – seeing the potential and seeing it change as they save it.

(Modern foreign languages – MFL 6)

Using the redrafting process allowed them to see that working with the technology was actually the key – it was a way of helping them see that what they were doing and learning was not separate from the technology – in fact, they couldn't redraft and save and see the gradual change without the menus.

(Modern foreign languages – MFL 4)

We thought that using hypertext might be a good way for linking poems and concepts together . . . I hope they can now see the links between texts more clearly because there was a physical link by clicking on a bit of text and taking you to an analysis of it. Or click on the text, and it takes you to something that was similar in another text. So they seemed to see the connections more clearly because of hyperlinks. This makes the teaching more powerful because the properties of the technology reinforce a way of teaching we use.

(English – ENG 7)

There was also evidence that some teachers were beginning to see new technologies as tools that could enable new forms of subject learning as well as loosening the constraints that often hindered deeper subject engagement and understanding. In a sense, they were alluding to the ways in which key relationships and structures within subject domains could be made more visible and the ways in which ICT facilitated that process (Noss and Hoyles 1996). They also commented that if learning goals were compromised, then ICT use became inhibited. In these instances, viewing technology as a mediating tool (Wertsch 1998) appeared to emphasise its invisibility, thus allowing subject learning to develop with limited technological obstacles. In this sense, the technology appeared to be integrated less problematically with the activities. However, some still expressed concern that too often software and hardware 'got in the way' and that it 'obstructed' or 'limited what kids should learn' as defined by the teacher. This bundle of issues tended to relate in the main to the students' need to 'tinker' with the technology and to 'go off task' too easily. This was most cogently expressed by one English teacher who felt:

> [T]hey are always bloody fiddling, and it irritates me because it gets in the way of learning. They are bloody obsessed with layout – it's underline in red and do the headings in 'neat' – the problem we had with exercise books, but it's on a larger scale because of all the possibilities for fiddling. I really stress that layout and presentation are secondary to content, but most are just obsessed.
>
> (English – ENG 1)

This reference to what Triggs and Matthewman (2003: 125) call 'obsessive compulsive font disorder' reflects Wenger's (1990) concept of cultural transparency and the ways in which the artefact can get in the way of understanding and learning because of the power of some of its more visible affordances. However, the levels of concern were relatively low, which implies a greater synergy between the transparency and opacity of the technology, thus improving its ability to facilitate subject-matter learning. This increase in synergy may also be related to extended and supportive frameworks.

A number of non-technological issues also emerged within the data that hindered the more extended use of ICT in the various subject areas. These included:

- the impact of assessment regimes;
- the constraints of timetabled access to technology;
- the tension between teacher control and pupil ownership of activities and learning;
- the need for pen and paper to provide evidence of learning or records for subsequent revision and reference – best characterised by the exercise book;
- the demand for a deeper understanding of exactly what involvement with technology appears to be contributing to learning;
- the problematic nature of the subject boundaries;
- the challenge of integrating ICT with the recommended procedures relating to the various national strategies for literacy and numeracy.

Activity

What things 'irritate' you when using or planning to use new technology in your teaching? What non-technological barriers emerge? List them in order of priority, starting with the most problematic, and work your way down.

Discussion

It can be concluded that many of the changes in practice taking place across the curriculum remained at the level of adaptation where new ideas and technologies were taken on board as long as higher-order intentions – learning and subject-based goals – were not overcompromised. In this sense, high levels of consonance with existing subjects and learning goals were sought. It also meant seeing the barriers between personal, home and school uses as permeable. At this point, the technology as a learning tool became more visible, but its role as a mediating technology less so.

In mathematics – a subject with a close traditional affiliation to new technologies – most teachers were comfortable with the deployment and use of ICT; however, some doubts were expressed about the potential loss of basic mathematical skills and thinking processes. In music, on the other hand, the teachers were more positive about the potential of new technologies to challenge both the performance and compositional base of the subject. For some, ICT amounted to a 'democratising tool' in that it allowed children with little traditional cultural capital in music to express their musicality with devices that connected to their own particular experiences. Finally, in modern foreign languages, there was the feeling that the generic software mirrored many of the needs of the subject and enhanced its semantic and syntactic features, although its limitations in terms of oral work were recognised.

The need for 'information discernment' (La Velle *et al.* 2004) was also highlighted in the interviews, as were the ongoing concerns about 'attention deficit', where many felt that the sheer speed of the technology and its constant interactivity might conspire to derogate what many called the 'traditional' skills of listening, watching, thinking and considering. Where this deficit appeared to be dominating subject learning, many teachers intervened to limit what they regarded as the 'distracting aspects of ICT' (Science – SCI 2). It was during this process of mediation that many of the teachers were able to blend their pedagogy with the recognisable potential offered by the technology in order to redirect attention onto the subject and its complexities. These findings are similar to those of Ruthven *et al.* (2004), who discovered that encouraging pupil reflection and criticality allowed the technology to play a greater mediating role in learning. They also noted that markedly contrasting subject profiles within the curriculum reflected corresponding differences in wider subject sub-cultures, in particular, the pedagogical discourses and practices that shape teachers' representations of ICT use (Ruthven *et al.* 2004). There was also evidence that teachers were becoming more aware of their own implicit theories about their subjects and the underlying pedagogy. In part, ICT encouraged this process of critical reflection and seemed to give a nudge to more challenging approaches to practice beyond the technology.

Crucially, the prominence of learning goals and the desire to maintain these underlying structures in the face of technological intrusion was a key feature. Ruthven *et al.* (2004) suggest that this implies a support role for ICT and the inevitability of assimilation process rather than accommodation and even transformation. The inference drawn, therefore, is that the maintenance of underlying learning goals is not necessarily limiting but instead facilitates the blending of technology with the curriculum that might eventually lead to greater transformation of practice. Furthermore, it highlights the evolutionary and the exploratory aspects of the interaction between subjects and ICT where teachers maintain their professional control over the technology using their 'pedagogic pragmatism' (Moore 2003) to decide when there is genuine resonance with subject philosophies. This idea of 'continuous evolution' is in contrast to the 'discontinuous processes' often put forward by many ICT advocates. Taking a cue from evolutionary theory (Dawkins 1998, 2003), we argue that the emphasis on more radical or discontinuous transformations of learning through ICT, where teachers are encouraged to put technology and innovation before their pedagogy (Watson 2001), might result in poor long-term integration. Instead, a continuous approach is advocated where technology and pedagogy evolve in a more seamless way.

Conclusion

The findings from the study reported in this chapter support what Watson (2001) terms a gradual shift in ICT thinking towards a 'pedagogic cultural agenda' where subject philosophies, pedagogical content knowledge and reflection are regarded as central characteristics. If this agenda is to materialise, then schools and subjects need time to adjust to using ICT, to explore its possibilities and to engage with its affordances as well as understanding its constraints. These conditions are dependent on a number of characteristics, all of which according to Eraut (2000) are regarded as fundamental to the creation of a suitable organisational micro-climate. They include:

- a blame-free culture;
- learning from experiences – positive and negative – at both group and individual levels;
- trying to make full use of the various knowledge resources held by members;
- encouraging talk about learning;
- locating and using relevant knowledge from outside the group;
- enhancing and extending understandings and capabilities of both the group as a whole and its individual members.

9 Constructing the digital classroom
Management of technological change in schools

Chapter overview

It has been said that the only certainty in life is that everything will change. Whether or not this is true, we are all acutely aware that change is a constant challenge, particularly within the teaching profession. Managing the process of technological change is a key survival skill teachers are acquiring as they face up to an uncertain future. The focus of this chapter is on change management and change agency, and will enable you to:

- examine concepts of the 'digital classroom';
- appreciate issues of change management and change agency;
- explore the notions of technology transparency, relevancy and usability;
- understand the role of the ICT coordinator as a change agent in the construction of digital learning environments.

Construction in progress

Any 'construction' of the 'digital classroom' should be seen as metaphorical. Today, with the rapid advance of new technologies, it is no longer vital to construct a physical 'place' or 'space' in which digitally mediated learning activities take place. It may also no longer be desirable, particularly where teachers feel that the 'computer room' has a disruptive influence on lesson continuity (see Chapter 8). Even the notion that learning must occur within a defined setting such as a school 'classroom' is now being challenged and may become increasingly redundant. It has been argued, for example, that the creation of ICT suites in which an array of computers is located more or less permanently, is a retrograde step, limiting mobility and activity of use (Muirhead 2005). ICT suites can also restrict learner access, creating problems with the day-to-day running of classes, as well as causing disruption when groups have to be moved between rooms (Watson 2001). Access to ICT suites may also be limited in many schools due to specialised classes such as ICT-skills sessions and the practice of block-booking facilities (Watson 2001). As we have previously articulated, the advent of ubiquitous computing has made it possible for learning to take place anywhere and at any time. Wireless technologies, handheld and mobile devices are increasingly accessible in education and will continue to grow in popularity as prices fall. For many schools, such digital resourcing may be unattainable in the short term due to the presently high costs. The strongest factor in perpetuation of ICT suites, however, is the perception of headteachers that 'this is the way it should be done'. Although we are living in the information age, where pervasive technologies, wireless connections and mobile devices are revolutionising access to content, it appears that ICT suites and classroom computers will be with us for some time to come. Traditional and digital classrooms, it seems, will continue to coexist side by side, sometimes overlapping, sometimes complementing each other.

For the purposes of this chapter then, we shall assume that the 'ICT suite' and the classroom equipped with ICT – that is, designated areas in which digital technology can be used to support and enhance learning – are what is meant by the term 'digital classroom'. We can also extend this notion to learning outside of the school, through the use of the home-based personal computer and the increased use by children of mobile technologies such as the cellular phone. In this chapter, it will be argued that successful construction of such environments requires knowledge of the technology, an understanding of the pedagogical implications and an appreciation of the psychological underpinning for its use.

Rising to the challenge

Establishing meaningful use of ICTs in schools can be a challenging prospect, not least because it has the potential to be divisive. Some teachers baulk at the idea. Teachers often need to change their teaching styles or repurpose their methods to integrate technology (Wheeler 2001), and for some teachers, this can be a step too far. Others are enthusiastic, but commitment tails off after a series of technical failures or bad experiences. There always appears to be a small percentage of 'lone rangers' who persevere and keep the technology alive. Yet, using ICT in the classroom is not a new practice. Teachers were using ICT long before the introduction of the computer. Any device that can be used to communicate, from chalkboard and slate, photocopy machines, 'magic lanterns' (what we once referred to as the 'epidiascope') and other projectors, radio and television broadcasting have all been used successfully (and sometimes not so successfully) by teachers down the years.

When I was still in primary school in the mid-1960s, I recall an occasion when it was arranged for us to watch a live educational television broadcast. It was quite an event for my classmates and me. Although many of us already had televisions in our homes, watching television at school was a great departure from the norm, as it had previously only been seen by us as 'entertainment'. Now, it was going to be used as a serious teaching tool, and we were going to watch it en masse. All of the children in my class were excited and captivated by the new experience.

Now, my son has followed me through the experience of primary school and, along the way, has regularly participated in the use of a number of new ICTs including wireless networked computers, broadband connection to the Internet and IWBs. He can skilfully use digital cameras to capture images and software to manipulate and organise them so they

---

Activity

Think back to your time in school. What technologies were used within your lessons? What did the technology do to enhance the lessons? What rules and considerations do you think were applied to its use? What were the expectations of the teacher and the students?

tell a story. His latest project, about the rainforests, contains his work in the form of integrated text, images and graphics, entirely generated through home and school personal computers. Technology has moved on from the monochrome television broadcasts of my day, but the general ethos of using ICT for educational purposes is still governed by the same principles and expectations.

Once a technology takes hold within a teaching culture, it begins to establish itself as a means through which the teacher not only *delivers* a lesson but begins to *reconceptualise* learning and teaching. IWBs, for example, are no longer simply display boards upon which the classroom teacher can write or present diagrams. They are now devices that can interface with dynamic learning resources such as hyperlinked websites, videos and animations. Teachers using these facilities must inevitably alter their approaches and change their methods to maximise the new features of the technology.

For the use of television in my own primary-school classroom, my teacher would have needed to apportion time, consider suitability for audience age and attainment levels, appraise the learning resource in the context of the curriculum of the day, check the availability of the technology, evaluate its effectiveness and familiarise herself with its operation. She would also have needed to formulate a 'Plan B' in case anything went wrong! Today, regardless of the increased sophistication and availability of ICT, teachers remain encumbered with the need to rationalise their use in teaching and learning contexts. Used effectively and creatively, technology still has the capacity to capture the attention and imagination of children of all ages and to inspire students to explore new ideas.

Resistance to change

However, as we indicated earlier in Chapter 2, when they are first introduced, many new technologies meet with resistance or apathy from some teachers (Wheeler and Winter 2005). Indeed, many promising technological innovations have stalled or met with failure, and there have been well-documented criticisms of the highly vaunted promises surrounding educational technology (Cuban 2001, Venezky 2004). Without wholesale adoption, many new technologies fail to find a foothold in the classroom, and schools are often left with equipment which gathers dust at the back of a cupboard in the staffroom. At least three key reasons for the failure of technology in schools have been identified. These are: limited opportunities for staff training during school hours; negative attitudes to ICT or a clash of teaching styles against the ICT; and limitations in technical support (Venezky 2004). Certainly, as Somekh has suggested, the introduction of ICT into a previously stable context often acts as a magnifying glass to amplify problems that are already endemic within teaching (Somekh 1992).

This same principle may apply as equally to large-scale implementation as it does to the individual classroom. In one large American learning technology evaluation project I worked on, full-motion video-conferencing systems were installed in classrooms, tested and demonstrated, training was provided, and then the teachers were expected to use them. Unsurprisingly, after a period of time, some systems were removed because they were never used. My team's research revealed that some teachers could see no imme-diate relevancy or need for the technology; others were fearful of using the devices; and some resented being told what to do in their own classrooms (Simonson *et al.* 2003). As is often the case, when 'new ideas' are imposed 'top-down' upon the teaching profession, resentment may result due to a clash between the symbolic function of technology within society and teachers' professional judgement and autonomy (Watson 2001). The problems of the US project demonstrate a waste of valuable resources and, perhaps even worse, an opportunity for transformation that has been squandered. When handled creatively and expertly, however, the management of technological change can reap benefits and enhance or transform the way in which the business of teaching and learning is conducted (Fox 2003). There are three premises upon which the success or failure of the introduction of a new technology into the classroom is reliant:

1   Technology must be relevant.
2   Technology must be transparent.
3   Technology must be supported.

Relevance of the technology

Teachers who do not see relevant uses for a new technology may reject it in favour of something else, generally returning to a 'tried and trusted' method or resource. Their time is at a premium, and they can ill afford to waste this time struggling to get a technology to work. Further, if they fail to see the relevance of the technology in terms of supporting learning, achieving curricular aims and outcomes or simply as a means to reduce the load and demand of mundane tasks throughout the day, the technology will not be adopted willingly. For some, technology may be perceived as being imposed from above as some kind of management exercise to increase efficiency. Others may simply oppose themselves to new technologies through moral or religious beliefs. Fundamentally, new technologies require a clear rationale for use based on clear pedagogical principles and sound evidence (Plowman *et al.* 2006) if teachers are to be motivated to use them. As Norman (1999) has offered, when technology is introduced, adoption is influenced the most by whether a task is important, valuable and cannot be done in any other way.

Technology transparency

Technology that is opaque and requires a lot of investment in time, mental energy and effort will be rejected in favour of something easier. On the other hand, technology that is transparent is easy to use and has little demands on the cognitive energy of the user. Transparent technology is often referred to as 'user friendly' in that it allows the user to 'see through' the device into what it is able to do for them (Wheeler 2000). All new technologies require some time and patience to master, as each is unfamiliar to the user, but, of course, some are easier to use than others. The design of a technology often has an impact on how quickly it becomes transparent, but it is often not until the second or third generation of a technology that it becomes user-friendly and the needs of the user subsume the design intentions of the manufacturer (Norman 1990).

   Another factor that impacts upon the transparency of the technology is the attitude of the user. Some teachers feel threatened by new technologies, either because they feel they cannot master the operation of the device or they feel embarrassed that some of the children in the classroom may know more about how to operate the technology than they do. Others feel positive about the potential of ICT to enhance their teaching but lack confidence. It is doubly important then that new technologies are easy to use, with a minimum of effort.

Technical support

In small primary schools, technical support is often provided by a teacher or parent on a part-time and sometimes ad hoc basis. Such an arrangement is at best sporadic and unreliable, with some equipment left unserviceable for long periods before it is repaired or replaced. Some problems, particularly complex ones such as network connectivity problems, may require specialised long-term support which can be expensive. Larger primary schools may be able to tap into funding to employ dedicated staff to manage technical infrastructures and maintain facilities. Most secondary schools and community colleges already have this infrastructure in place.

Technical support is becoming increasingly vital as schools establish internal networks, create web presence and explore new ways of functioning such as school–home links and wireless operation. Increasingly, schools are taking advantage of the 'lease-hire' schemes offered by larger computer companies, where suites of networked computers are installed, on-site maintenance and support hotlines are provided, and the entire suite is replaced with new equipment at the end of a pre-agreed time period. It is evident that teachers will need to adapt to new technologies, but, even more importantly, it is clear that schools will need to create efficient and responsive organisational systems in which technology is technically managed and sustained.

Where it all goes wrong

Technology that is in poor state of repair or that proves to be unreliable is naturally rejected in favour of something that is more dependable. However, reliability does not always depend on the condition of the technology. Usually, when shiny new technology is installed in a classroom, it is in pristine condition and should function according to the manufacturer's specifications. Yet, provision does not always account for issues such as compatibility, the need of a 'fit for purpose' statement or usability levels.

Another set of issues influencing the success or failure in adoption of a new technology can be found in the planning process. If the school management has failed to fully consider how the technology will be supported in the long term in areas such as training, upgrading, maintenance and repair, problems are likely to arise. We have examined support and shall examine each of the other issues in turn.

Compatibility

Issues of compatibility have often confounded the effective use of technology in schools. There are many stories of teachers who returned from holiday in the USA with a very useful VHS videotape that had 'great educational content'. The disappointment came when they attempted to play the tape on the school video machine and then realised that the American video standard NTSC (National Television Systems Committee) was not compatible with the British video standard PAL (Phase Alternation Line). Thankfully, with the advent of DVD, these problems have been all but eradicated. However, teachers should still be aware that televisions in the UK operate on a different basis to those in some other countries, so the use of video can still be riddled with problems.

Computer software is another area of compatibility concern. Issues of 'backwards' compatibility have often thwarted an otherwise well-planned lesson, specifically when teachers have used a newer version of a particular software package at home to create an eye-catching, inspirational teaching resource only to be disappointed when they try to run it in class and discover that the older version of the software installed on the school network does not accept the new file. Many PowerPoint presentations have been spoiled in this way, where the text font style created at home does not translate on the school computer, because the teacher forgot to save as a 'pack and go' version. There are many little irregularities and hidden pitfalls of compatibility which teachers should be aware of when using ICT. A simple maxim should be learned by all those who wish to avoid embarrassment and disappointment: plan, prepare and practise.

'Fit for purpose'

This term is one heard increasingly within education circles. Consider the following definition of 'fit for purpose':

> Fit for Purpose is a general expression which can be useful to ensure that Information [. . .] solutions are appropriate for your organisation. Vendors will sometimes attempt to 'fit' their solution to your problem. Fit for Purpose is an expression which, when used within the solution negotiation context, places an onus of responsibility upon the vendor to ensure that its solution is (indeed) fit for the purpose which their client expects.
>
> (Fit for Purpose)

It appears that this definition of 'fit for purpose' technology results from a clear, purpose-driven negotiation between providers and clients. In an educational context, this will typically be the vendor and the local education authority or, in some cases, the vendor and the school direct.

I once observed a teaching practice in a junior school where a new data projector was connected to a wall-mounted IWB. The school had purchased the equipment so that lessons could be enhanced through the much-heralded new technology. The teachers had done their research and had discovered that whiteboard technologies could offer learners a visual, auditory and kinaesthetic experience that tapped into all of the pre-dominant learning styles of the pupils.

What they had not considered, however, was that each time the data projector was removed from its cupboard and set up on the desk, it needed to be 'oriented' – set up so that the projector was registered correctly with the computer. Each time a pupil walked past the table and knocked it ever so slightly, the projector would move minutely, and the whole system would be out of alignment. This required the teacher to realign the projector with the screen approximately half a dozen times during a fifty-minute lesson, wasting valuable time, frustrating pupils and teaching staff alike and generally eroding any of the intrinsic benefits of the new technology.

Such mundane issues often mar an otherwise well-conceived plan. The technology did not match the pedagogy, and its configuration was not fit for purpose. Through a little better planning, and the investment of a few extra pounds, the data projector could have been ceiling mounted and all of the technical problems eradicated. This was an example of a new device that was 'fit for purpose' but was not utilised effectively due to lack of supporting structure.

Usability

Teachers need to ask how usable an ICT is. Originally, personal computers were designed to be used by adults in business contexts. They had not been conceived of as being used by children in a learning situation. Hence, their size, fixed position and other ergonomic factors such as the fine motor control and hand–eye coordination needed to effectively operate the mouse, means that smaller children can sometimes find it difficult to use a computer properly (Plowman *et al.* 2006). Further, children often fail to ask for help when they need it, so it is important that teachers closely monitor children's use of personal computers and are able to intervene to provide support where it is necessary.

Another aspect of usability is the amount of fun and enjoyment the children can derive from the use of ICT. Teachers need to be aware that personal computers are simply one part of the equation. Other ICTs such as digital cameras, video camcorders, mobile phones and PDAs can all provide learners with opportunities to be creative, offer mobility and an almost endless number of collaborative possibilities. Children can quickly become very competent in their use, and the obvious added value is that they can develop valuable skills which are transferable into the world of work.

Diffusion of innovation

There are thought to be four discrete stages of diffusion when a new technology is first introduced into a classroom (Mandinach and Cline 1994). The first, known as *survival*, is fairly clear in its meaning. In the survival stage, teachers struggle to define what it is they can achieve with the new technology and attempt to learn how to use it effectively. They grapple with its functionality and, in so doing, begin to assess whether they can actually use it. The second stage, *mastery*, is where teachers begin to move beyond surviving to use the technology in meaningful situations, and the technology begins to become transparent to the user. The third stage, known as *impact*, is evaluative, requiring users to appraise the extent to which the technology is being effective and how they are coping with any problems that have arisen through its use. The final stage, and perhaps the most important, is the *innovation* stage, in which teachers begin to use the technology in new and creative ways, to achieve outcomes that would previously have been unreachable. According to Venezky, this final stage is recognisable by the number of restructured learning activities that occur within the classroom and the extent to which these enhance best practice. Schools in which the fourth stage of diffusion has been reached are staffed by teachers who feel free to adapt ICT to their own style of teaching (Venezky 2004).

Innovation diffusion is a field of enquiry with a long and illustrious history. In his seminal work on the adoption of innovation, Everitt Rogers defines key groups of people who fall into the camps of innovators, early adopters and early or late majority, who adopt innovation at various stages of its evolution. There are also 'laggards' who are particularly reticent in their adoption of a new idea and possibly those who may simply resist it or attempt to subvert it (see Figure 9.1). Rogers provides socio-economic profiles for each grouping and argues that it is the innovators who are the most instrumental in the success of a new idea (Rogers 1983).

Applying this model to the uptake of new technologies in the UK, we can see that some technologies have penetrated society to such an extent that their impact on education is significant. Between 2000 and 2005, there was a dramatic rise in the ownership of personal computers by families with school-age children, and the percentage now stands at around 76 per cent (Figure 9.2). For terrestrial television, the figure is nearer to 100 per cent, but

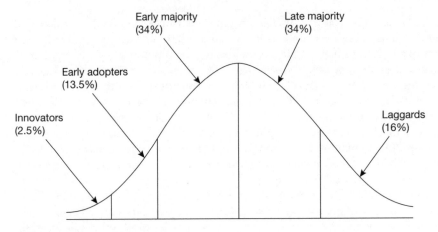

Figure 9.1 Diffusion of innovations model.
Source: Adapted from Rogers (1983).

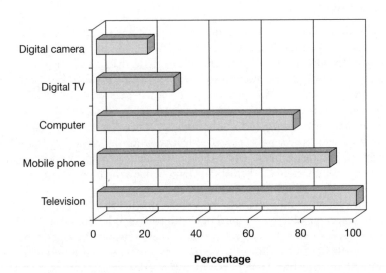

Figure 9.2 Diffusion of technologies in families with school-age children (2005).
Source: National Statistics Office (2005).

for digital television, a newer technology, only 30 per cent of families with school-age children have so far bought in, presumably due to the added cost of satellite or cable subscription. Mobile telephones account for 90 per cent of the market, whilst digital cameras own approximately just a 20 per cent share (Sefton-Green 2005).

The virtuous circle

As economies of scale in the manufacture of new technology become more efficient, two things happen. Production costs are reduced and support networks proliferate. As more people buy into the product, so newer, sleeker, smarter and cheaper versions are produced.

This virtuous circle sustains both production and wider use, thereby enabling the technology to gain a firmer foothold for itself within society. The deeper a technology penetrates, the more people's perceptions are influenced by it. In an ideal world, school managers would take heed of these adoption trends and adjust their resource provision accordingly to meet the perceptions and expectations of teaching professionals and young people alike. It also follows that the construction of any digital learning resource will quickly become outmoded unless regular upgrades are made as technological trends progress.

Without a clear picture of the way people embrace new ideas, companies would fail to understand the need of professional bodies and communities of practice such as the teaching profession and would manufacture unwanted products. This has happened on many occasions. One memorable example was the invention, design and production of Sinclair's electric car – the C5. A case study of the C5 is presented below.

Case study: the Sinclair C5

Sir Clive Sinclair was well known for his revolutionary designs of electronic gadgets and products. Sinclair Research Ltd successfully marketed a number of innovations including pocket calculators, portable televisions (1975), micro-computers (1980) and one of the first available home computers, the popular ZX Spectrum (1982).

On the back of the successful manufacture and marketing of his miniature television and Spectrum computer, it seemed a natural progression for him to attempt the design of an electric car – the Sinclair C5. In the 1970s, green issues began to loom large in public consciences, which encouraged the British government to pass a law that allowed non-taxed use of the environmentally friendly electric motorcycle.

Sir Clive saw his opportunity but met with dissent from his board of directors, and so he took the drastic step of selling off a proportion of his company shares. This raised a reported £12 million to finance his project. Lotus agreed to design the chassis of the C5; Polymotor manufactured the engine; and the vehicle was constructed at the Hoover factory in Wales.

Unfortunately, the C5 launch was held in the middle of the cold winter of 1985, and the vehicles were less than impressive on the icy roads, skidding and handling badly. The media were highly critical, and Sinclair received a great deal of bad press. The road safety standards organisations took an interest, and public confidence was damaged. After a brief flurry of interest, sales of the C5 plummeted to zero, production was halted, and the company closed its book the same year. It was estimated that Sir Clive lost the sum of £8.6 million on this venture.

(Adapted from www.microcarmuseum.com/tour/sinclair-c5.html).

So, what happened to make the launch of the Sinclair C5 a disaster? Consider the following facts:

- The launch of the Sinclair C5 appeared to usher in a new era of ecologically friendly personal transport, and many were excited at the prospect of buying an electric vehicle for an affordable £399. Underage drivers could legally drive them, and C5 owners required no licence, road tax or motor insurance. They didn't require petrol, so drivers could save money on travel and be ecologically responsible at the same time.

- On the downside, the C5 needed to use heavy batteries which were unreliable. This meant that the Sinclair C5 wasn't quite as liberating as many hoped it would be. Drivers needed to use built-in pedals to start the vehicle or to climb up steep hills. The manufacturer claimed that the range of the C5 was 20 miles on a single battery charge, but the designers had failed to take Britain's cold winter weather into account. Cold snaps drastically reduced the performance of the battery. Another problem with the battery was the length of time (at around eight hours) which was required to charge it up. Many C5 users, therefore, had to purchase a second battery.
- The C5 was very low on the road, so safety concerns were an issue. C5 drivers were not required by law to wear a crash helmet, so the potential for serious injury was significant.

For these reasons, the Sinclair C5 was doomed to failure. Car owners were not keen on the 'downgrade' to an electric vehicle, so kept their cars. Cyclists refused to change to an electric vehicle for a variety of reasons, and motorcyclists thought the top speed (at around 15 miles per hour) was simply laughable. Although the C5 enjoyed a brisk start to its sales (1,000 sales in the first week), customers soon deserted Sinclair, and the company was eventually wound up.

(Adapted from http://homepages.enterprise.net/cavan/ysac/c5.shtml.)

Activity

Reflect on the previous case study. What do you consider were the key reasons for the failure of the C5?

Lessons to be learned

We can learn an important lesson from the failure of innovations such as the Sinclair C5 and apply them to the school context. Issues such as the need for technology that is fit for purpose and applications that enhance or extend, rather than duplicate, current practice are paramount. Ease of use and transparency of purpose are also key requirements for the success of technological change management.

Ultimately, diffusion of new technology throughout a school requires strong leadership, good modelling and a prolonged exposure of staff and students to the ICT. There are four key rules if implementation is to be successful.

1   Innovations must be professionally led.
2   Innovations must be expertly modelled.

3   Innovations must be embedded into practice.
4   Innovations must have cross-curricular applications.

A useful list of practical tips is offered below for schools that wish to construct their own 'digital classrooms'.

- Don't be seduced by the technology and think you've got to get the latest and best – make the most of what you have first.
- Don't rush – plan strategically, considering purchase, training, implementation and development costs over a long period.
- Don't invest in expensive software unless you have the time and resources to develop its application.
- Talk to others and share the lessons they've learnt.
- Don't worry that the students know more about ICT than you – learn from them!
- Don't bury your head in the sand – ICT is here to stay, so learn to live with it and move forward.
- Think carefully about how ICT can be used to enhance the quality of students' outcomes.
- Test innovations at the top of the school then introduce them with the youngest children.
- Invest time in teaching the skills necessary to use your current ICT applications to their best advantage.
- Prepare guidance booklets to allow the students to develop independent learning skills.
- Provide a range of output devices to maximise the use of your ICT applications.
- Consider carefully where your ICT hardware will be located to keep it clean and safe and allow it to enhance your learning environment.
- Ensure that decisions are made as part of the whole-school approach to ICT.
- Make best use of your current ICT resources.
- At the same time, invest in the future in terms of money, time and staff training.

(The Design and Technology Association,
http://web.data.org.uk/data/secondary/crosscurr_ict.php)

To construct an effective and sustainable digital learning environment, all of the above principles need to be adhered to and the practical tips considered. Strong ICT leadership is also required to ensure that clear guidance and direction are given to those involved in the construction.

The role of the ICT coordinator

Within UK schools, such professional management and decision-making is usually the remit of the ICT coordinator. This individual is likely to be a teacher within the school who is the most adept at using ICTs or who has exhibited the keenest interest in them for a while (although this is not always the case). Essentially, ICT coordinators are potential change agents. Within a profession where change is rapid and relentless, ICT coordinators find themselves at the centre of a maelstrom of acute technological change, requiring them to acquire the ability to be flexible and adaptable and the skill to anticipate new trends. If they become expert modellers (or, in Rogers' terms, 'opinion leaders'), they will be very effective in influencing the behaviour of their colleagues and may ultimately contribute towards the successful uptake of the new technology. At the very least, they will be expected to embed new technologies into their own professional practice and be seen by their colleagues to champion the new technology across the entire curriculum.

At the time of writing, it appears that few ICT coordinators are being appointed specifically to fulfil these kinds of roles in UK schools. Often, newly appointed ICT co-ordinators find themselves taking on ill-defined or self-specified roles and creating niches for themselves within them. Few are given clear job descriptions that define what an ICT coordinator should do, possibly because many schools have little idea about the direction their ICT strategy will take, and fewer still can completely and accurately predict what their ICT needs will be. One role of the ICT coordinator is clear, however, and this is to promulgate the use of ICT across all areas of the curriculum and to embed it within all activities of the life of the school. ICT coordinators will also take a strong lead in the training and professional updating of teaching staff. Where this vital role is left unfulfilled, schools tend to lag far behind the current wave of take-up of new ICT.

Conclusion

The introduction of new technologies into conservative settings such as the traditional school classroom can be severely inhibited if the cultural climate is hostile. Teacher attitudes towards technology are influenced by a number of factors, including perceptions of relevancy, transparency and ease of use and whether there is enough support if and when things go wrong. Teachers also require strong leadership, training and modelling if they are to see clear links between innovation and practice. It is evident that to successfully construct a digital learning environment of any kind, whether physically or virtually, a clear rationale for use is required, based on sound pedagogical principles and empirical evidence. Schools that adopt ICT to extend the boundaries of the traditional classroom may struggle at times to achieve success, but if that small success is able to be sustained over a period of time and strong support is found within the ranks of the teaching staff, then the potential for transformation of the learning experience for all students will be a likely outcome.

10 Connecting the learning community
Extending classroom boundaries

Chapter overview

We argued in the previous chapter that schools are in a process of change. Some of the changes are driven by the ways in which schools relate to the community and, specifically, how teachers and parents communicate. There is increasing encouragement for schools to link their activities to home life, providing students with a seamless learning experience that transcends traditional boundaries. In the chapter you will:

- explore the concept of home–school links;
- learn about the concepts of m-learning and u-learning;
- assess the contribution of digital technology to home–school linking;
- evaluate the use of mobile technologies in learning.

One charity in the UK, Tools for Schools, specialises in the recycling of old, unwanted personal computers. It offers them at cut price to schoolchildren and their families, as well as teachers and teaching assistants. In 2004, this scheme received support from the then Secretary of State for Education, Charles Clarke.

In 2005, a London School of Economics study claimed that 'Internet illiterate' parents could disadvantage their children and harm their prospects. Middle-class parents who are unable to support their children's use of computers at home are an increasing factor in the nation's growing digital divide. In the study, 1,511 nine to nineteen year olds and 906 of their parents were asked about their Internet use. Ninety-eight per cent of the children had access to the Internet, either at home, school or elsewhere. Twenty per cent had access to the Internet in their bedrooms, but another 25 per cent of the sample only had access to the Internet at school.

Introduction

The examples above are indicative of a growing awareness that computer technologies have the capability to support the distribution of learning activities across home and school. Increasingly, the relentless march of technology is beginning to blur traditional boundaries between school and home such that it is no longer tenable to claim that the learning exclusively takes place within the school. Indeed, this has never been the case, but, influenced by the industrial age, in which learning was formalised, synchronised and conducted predominantly within the setting of the classroom, public perception has been that 'school is the place where you learn'. Now all of this is about to change.

Today, Internet-linked computers at home and school, coupled with mobile technologies, can create an overlapping dynamic and virtual environment within which students can create, store, retrieve and make use of learning resources. In this chapter, we explore some of the possibilities, influences, affordances and constraints of ICT-supported learning and its contribution towards extending the boundaries of learning beyond the school.

The medium of media

The Internet is now the centrally most important learning technology. It is a global phenomenon and has also been called the 'medium of media', because it embraces radio, television, images, textbooks, telephone and e-mail communication – in fact, almost every other medium that has gone before it (Levinson 2003). Through the Internet, children have the opportunity to access digital learning resources anywhere and at any time.

The London School of Economics study referenced on p. 105 is indicative of an interesting trend. Three out of four children no longer rely solely on school provision to access the Internet, whilst one in five children enjoy Internet access within their own bedroom. Never before has the world of learning been so open and available to so many young minds, and in such a personalised and flexible manner. The data are also indicative of another trend, perhaps one that should concern LEAs and teachers alike. It is that one in four children still do not have home access to networked resources and communication – a digital divide across the UK's youth population that differentiates between home and school use. Most LEAs would espouse the idea that children should be able to access and use the same learning resources regardless of their location, and many would agree there should be a seamless and adequate provision for all.

Bridging the digital divide

Problems arise for children of families that are not connected to the Internet, or who do not have a computer at home. As we have seen, although this is no longer the norm in the United Kingdom, there is still a small percentage of school-age children who have no access to the Internet outside of school. Even when top-of-the-range computers and broadband Internet connections do exist in a family home, it may be difficult or even impossible for children to access them, for a variety of reasons.

Activity

List reasons why some family homes may not have access to Internet-linked computers. What reasons might prevent children from using Internet-connected computers even when there is one in the home? Can you think of other problems that may cause inequity of ICT access for children at home?

Networked computers also offer greater potential for teachers and parents of children to communicate more effectively in a range of purposes (Becta 2005). Yet, there are many reasons some families do not have computers or other technology within their homes. Some families may simply not be able to afford the purchase price or may have a computer in the house but are unable to afford or justify a connection to an Internet service provider (ISP). Some families refuse to have Internet-connected computers in their homes because of religious, moral or cultural objections. Others may simply see no need for such technology in their home.

We should also be aware that there are travellers and families who have no permanent place to live for whom access to computers and the Internet is difficult or impossible. It could be argued that these are disadvantaged individuals because they are 'information poor' in an information-rich society. This is referred to as the 'digital divide' – a distinction between those who have access to ICT at home, and those who have not.

Computers in the home

The digital divide is not created solely by socio-economic drivers. Other factors contribute towards uneven access to ICT between home and school. Some remote rural areas of the UK are yet to be connected to broadband communication systems, and for these residents, fast access to the Internet can be problematic. This issue has been discussed at length in a number of recent articles and government papers (see, for example, Becta 2001) and has serious implications for inclusion, equality and the widening of participation in education.

Where computers do exist in the home, it may still be difficult for children to gain access, as for some families, the parents' use takes precedence. In some homes, parents maintain sole or dominant access to the computer and the Internet, particularly if a business is run from home. Further, parents may choose to restrict a child's access to the Internet to certain hours of the day or for set periods of time.

Parents may also prevent their children from using the Internet due to considerations of safety and privacy. They may view the computer as more of a threat than a benefit, due to media coverage of disturbing stories where young children have had intimate conversations with undesirable or dangerous individuals in chatrooms. They may also have concerns about the amount of pornographic, violent, racist or otherwise objectionable websites that exist in profusion on the Internet.

In a recent study, 41 per cent of UK parents admitted to checking their child's Internet activities, whereas in the USA closer to two-thirds of parents expressed a similar concern (BBC News, 28 April 2005). Eighty-six per cent of UK parents in the same sample stated that they would not allow their children to give personal information over the Internet, compared with only half of European parents. Some of these concerns are, of course, entirely justified, so one of the new roles of the teacher may be to educate parents into acceptance of ICT as a powerful, and – when used responsibly with appropriate guidelines – a safe educational tool.

Case study

Dawn is a teacher of English in a large rural secondary school. The school is well equipped with standard ICT suites, multimedia facilities, broadband connections and newer technologies such as IWBs and handheld computers in many of the classrooms. Recently, she decided to launch a project with her Year 8 students, studying television soap operas. Her aims were to ask the students to compare and contrast two television soaps, and create a fact sheet about the genre of television soaps. The learning outcome for this activity in the English Key Stage 3 scheme of work was stated as: 'Identifying and commenting on writers' purposes and viewpoints and overall effect of the text on the reader'. In the medium of television, the 'text' is moving and visual (the television script) and the 'reader' is of course the viewer.

Two sisters within the same class informed the teacher that they had no computer or television at home and were, therefore, unable to participate in the project. Their parents held the belief that the girls should be encouraged to read more to develop their literacy skills and that television and computers were a distraction.

Activity

Place yourself in the teacher's position. What alternative activities could you provide for the two girls that would produce equivalent learning outcomes? What media do the alternative activities rely upon?

The key to this activity is found in the wording of the learning outcome, which states that *text* is to be analysed by the *reader*. One alternative medium to use, therefore, would be any text-based medium such as a play or a novel.

Technophobia

Other digital divides can be constructed psychologically. Some people have an aversion to the use of technology, manifested in a spectrum of behaviour from intense fear to mild frustration or anger. Technophobic behaviour is manifested in how much a person 'will' or 'will not' use computers – another form of the digital divide (Wheeler and Winter 2005). Technophobia can be defined as a 'fear or anxiety towards computers' (Jay 1981: 47) and usually results in some form of avoidance behaviour.

Activity

List some factors you think might contribute to someone being technophobic.

Adverse responses to computers and the Internet may be based upon bad previous experiences or on fears that the computer will either be damaged or important data lost. For some teachers, it is possible that computers will be rejected simply because no immediate need of the technology is perceived. Moreover, it is possible that teachers may reject technology because they find it simply too difficult to use or that it takes too long to learn to use effectively. Donald Norman has written extensively in this area, claiming that computers are not designed to be 'transparent' to users and calling for a more user-centred approach to the manufacture of ICT (Norman 1999).

However they are viewed, user responses to ICT cannot be said to be completely free from negative attitudes towards the technology. Children can be just as susceptible to technophobia as adults, even though it has been argued that children may have more of an affinity for new technologies than older people (Prensky 2001). Moreover, technophobia may not necessarily be determined by age, as older people have been found in some studies to hold more positive attitudes to new technologies than younger people (Dyck and Smither 1994, Wheeler 2000). Brosnan suggests that such findings may be due to younger computer users being expected to be more computer literate, resulting in greater anxiety to perform (Brosnan 1998). We should, therefore, exercise caution in assuming that all children will be free from technophobia.

A broader discussion of the topic of technophobia and technology adoption is offered by Wheeler and Winter (2005) and a deeper treatment of psychological issues is presented by Brosnan (1998). We also revisit this topic in Chapter 12 in relation to models of teaching, literacy and orality. Often, technophobic responses to ICT lead to people refusing to use computers or severely curtailing their use. The number of lost opportunities to exploit the huge potential of ICTs may never be known, nor will its impeding of the development of information and communication skills.

Linking school and home

So, why should we link the school and the home? Strictly, the school has never existed in a vacuum. There have always been bridges between the school and its local community, at both micro and macro levels. Children bring homework back to the home to work on in the evenings and weekends, a simple method of extending the hours of learning beyond the walls of the formal classroom. Not only does the school come into the home but the home can also go to the school. Parents are invited to participate in the running of the school in a number of capacities, including, for example, parent-governorship, volunteer classroom support, part-time or unpaid work supporting ICT provision and fundraising activities through the Parent Teacher Association. These examples show that there have always been links between home and school, but there are, of course, also links between school and business/industry and the wider community. Teaching children must be seen as a partnership between all stakeholders. It is expedient then, that schools maintain and strengthen their ties with the outside world, looking outwards as well as inwards.

The UK government has already recognised the need to formalise partnership agreements between schools and parents. The Home School Agreement aims to build on existing relationships between school and home through the promotion of better communication about pupil progress, domestic concerns that may affect a child's attainment and homework. Parents and teachers are also encouraged to work together to address issues of social concern such as bullying, behaviour management and drug education (DfES

2006c). As we shall see in the following section, digital technology clearly has a role to play in the management of this initiative.

Examples of ICT-mediated home–school links

Using e-mail

One of the most obvious uses of digital technology in the connection of homes and schools must surely be e-mail. E-mail has been used so successfully within business and education in the past decade that it has become a key fabric of communication in our society. Without it, many of us would probably feel a little lost. Schools are increasingly using e-mail to communicate to governors, LEAs and, of course, parents and guardians.

Activity

What do you consider to be the advantages of using e-mail to communicate to parents? And what are the possible disadvantages?

A clear advantage to using e-mail to communicate to a large population of people such as parents is that a broadcast e-mail can be sent to an entire mail list on a single click of the mouse, in an efficient manner, so that all members receive the same information at the same time. This can obviate problems caused by 'rumour factory' or 'Chinese whispers' situations, where one parent hears slightly different information to his or her neighbour. There is also an archive of the message sent so that checking back on what was said by the school should be a simple task. Another pragmatic, economic advantage is that e-mail can help schools to avoid excessive postal charges or the sometimes 'hit and miss' communication method, where teachers ask young children to take an envelope home to their parents. Instantaneity of message sending and receipt can eliminate unnecessary delay of announcement of important news or information. Attachments of important documents, such as newsletters, images or other files, can also be sent at the same time.

There are also disadvantages to e-mail. The most serious constraint is that not all parents have access to, or wish to use, e-mail, so sending out broadcast messages could potentially exclude some children. Also, some parents may be omitted from the school's mailing list, excluding them from important information. Schools also need to acknowledge that some parents may prefer to communicate with the school through more traditional methods such as telephone or written letter or may prefer to meet with the teacher face to face.

Creating web presence

The Internet will play an increasingly vital role in the linking of school with home, and school web pages will be a central component. A very high percentage of schools in Western industrialised nations now have some form of web presence. The 'school website' is being used for an increasing number of purposes, which, for many, includes marketing of the school, dissemination of news and views, celebration of the school's achievements, communication between the school and the community and, perhaps most vitally, it is the organ through which an increasing amount of school–home connections are being made. Term dates, prospectus information and contact details are the most common items offered through this medium. A few schools are also beginning to use their websites as simple digital repositories for teaching and learning materials, although, at present, this is limited. Some enterprising teachers are creating their own websites to house and showcase teaching materials, schemes of work and digital learning resources they have developed, but these are generally outside of official school provision.

It must also be emphasised that schools should not enter lightly into the creation of websites. A website is like a newborn baby. Once it is brought into the world (wide web), it requires a great deal of continuing care and attention. Without regular feeding and changing, a baby will quickly become ill. Websites also need to be nurtured, or they will, inevitably, fail. They quickly go out of date, so require regular updating. Visitors to websites want to know how useful the web resources will be for them personally. If the site is out of date, with broken hyperlinks and containing old information or obsolete ideas, visitors will quickly leave and will not return. Successful websites tend to be dynamic, constantly updated and easy to navigate. A trawl through the school websites in your own region or community will demonstrate the varying quality and utility of school sites.

Activity

Visit some local school websites whilst asking the following questions:

- How does the site represent the school?
- What features are useful to you as a potential parent?
- What features are interesting to you?
- What features are in need of updating?
- If you were the webmaster of the site what would you change?

What other questions would you ask to ascertain the quality of the website? Make an evaluation of your own school website. How does it measure up to the best and worst of other school websites?

The role of mobile technology

It is our contention that mobile technologies will play an increasingly important role in strengthening connections between home and school. The spectacular recent rise in the use of mobile technologies across the Western world, particularly for school-age children, has meant that interpersonal communication has reached a new level. Recent UK government statistics reveal that mobile phones are now owned by 78 per cent of the population (National Statistics Office 2005), with more than a million in the hands of children between the ages of five and nine years – a third of the children in this age group (Futurelab 2005). The scene is set for a rapid upturn in the use of mobile technologies in formal education because they are flexible, children find them exciting and easy to use and they also have a great potential to transform the experience of learning that can be conducted at any time and in any place.

In the current information age, by the time a child reaches the age of twenty-one, he or she will have:

- sent over 200,000 text messages;
- played 10,000 hours of video games;
- watched over 20,000 hours of television;
- talked 10,000 hours on mobile phones;
- seen over 500,000 television adverts;
- spent less than 5,000 hours reading.

(Prensky 2001)

One of the remarkable facts about this set of statistics is that at the time of writing, it is already five years out of date. We can only project a trend from this, but assuming that mobile technologies and other media continue to proliferate, the hours spent on the activities listed above should rise accordingly. What remains to be seen is whether average hours spent reading are on the decline or whether they will rise in the light of the recent commercial success of children's books such as *Lord of the Rings*, the *Chronicles of Narnia* and the *Harry Potter* series.

Two of the six statistics above refer to the use of mobile phones – the new technological wave. A quick glance at Figure 10.1 informs us that between 2001 and 2003 there was a steady rise in the ownership of mobile phones in the United Kingdom and that ownership gravitates towards the youth of the nation.

Teachers and mobile technologies

Educational change is often driven by technological innovation, so teachers should be alive to the possibilities new technologies bring. Strengthening the links between school and

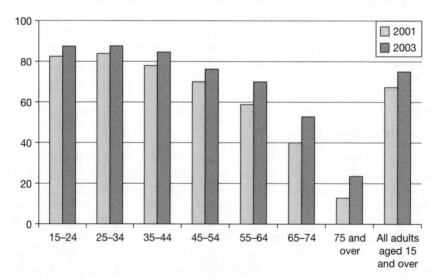

Figure 10.1 Rise in UK mobile-phone ownership between 2001 and 2003.
Source: Government's National Statistics Online, http://www.statistics.gov.uk/statbase/expodata/spreadsheets/d7202.csv.

home learning through the use of wireless technologies such as the mobile phone is an obvious progression. In effect, mobile devices have the potential to extend the learning environment beyond school and home, into any location. For some time, one of the most sought-after possibilities has been 'any time, any place' or ubiquitous learning (u-learning). For the first time, teachers may now be at the threshold of witnessing this as a reality.

New technologies have already driven many recent changes in colleges and universities. Now, it is the turn of the compulsory education sector. Some changes have had a deep impact because, as we have already emphasised, the introduction of new technology into the classroom has the potential to change not only the way education is conducted but, more fundamentally, also the manner in which it is conceptualised. The traditional teacher–pupil relationship, long premised on the expert–novice model, has been gradually eroded through a widening acceptance of social constructivist approaches to education. Interactive technologies have been brought to bear on the business of teaching and learning, providing some of the necessary social scaffolding required to support personalised construction of knowledge. Arguably, the expert–novice model has also been inadvertently undermined by children arriving in the classroom knowing more about new technologies than their teachers.

At the forefront of the most recent technology-driven changes, we find the mobile (cellular) telephone. Although many schools in the United Kingdom have already banned mobile phones for reasons of child safety (e.g. so-called 'happy-slapping' incidents), cheating and general classroom disruption, they are here to stay and are playing an increasingly important role in young people's lives. Teachers now need to seriously consider the impact that mobile phones will have on future education provision and begin to make plans to utilise them effectively. The following section of this chapter provides an insight into the scope of the phenomenon.

Surveys show that today's youth, and particularly those from ethnic minorities, are increasingly using mobile phones as a substitute for the personal computer. Using mobiles in this manner heralds a move towards ubiquitous computing. Such research reveals that having the power of a computer in the hand, wherever one goes, has an obvious appeal to young people. Such youth movements shape future trends and are fair indicators of what can be expected.

As with many successful diffusions of technology into society, adoption by youth sectors has driven the spectacular proliferation of mobile communication. The personal computer and the CD achieved success on the back of high percentages of youth purchase, and the same is now being witnessed in the mobile phone and ubiquitous computing sectors.

Consider some recent global statistics:

- More than 1 trillion text messages were sent via mobile phones worldwide in 2005.
- Over 1 billion mobile phones were purchased worldwide in 2006 (812 million were sold in 2005).
- The mobile phone is now the most commonly purchased electronic device worldwide.
- Mobile telephony is the fourth window of content after television, cinema and the personal computer.

The UK has one of the highest ownerships of mobile phones per head of population: in 2006 mobile-phone ownership in the UK topped 45 million, or about 84 per cent of the population. It is worth noting that this figure represents the number of unique mobile owners rather than actual mobile-phone accounts. Rather than attempting to sell subscriptions to the remaining 16 per cent of the population, the UK mobile-phone industry's long-term plan is to maintain growth of data and optimisation of profit through existing customers.

Nonetheless, the above statistic should be tempered with the reality that many mobile-phone users purchase more than one device, and some of the more avid users upgrade to newer and smarter mobile phones on a regular basis.

> 396 billion minutes of calls (equivalent to about two hours a week for every person in the UK) were made from fixed and mobile phone links in 2003. We can be assured that this statistic has grown in the intervening years. Additionally, 21.3 billion text messages were sent, or an equivalent to seven text messages per person per week.
>
> (http://www.statistics.gov.uk/pdfdir/yearbook1104.pdf)

Even in Third World countries, where over half the population have never made a fixed-line telephone call, the mobile telephone is gaining a strong foothold, to the extent that computer luminaries are debating its future impact.

Nick Negroponte of MIT had a radical idea to supply $100 laptops to children in Africa. However, this vision has been criticised by Microsoft CEO Bill Gates who argues that the enhanced connectivity provided by mobile phones will prove to be of greater value than laptops. Gates claims that a single mobile-phone mast has the capacity to connect a whole town and that mobile-phone users can access the web, send text and e-mail messages. It is evident that the mobile phone is assuming much of the essential functionality of the laptop computer.

So, exactly what is the appeal of the mobile phone for young people? One perspective is provided by Professor Anne Charlton of the University of Manchester, who believes that mobiles are marketed in a very similar way to cigarettes, with subtle nuances that focuses on self-image, identity and confidence. There is nothing illegal about such marketing strategies, but mobile-phone advertising tends to be very effective and seductive.

The dark side of mobiles

We have alluded to the fact that many UK schools have outlawed the use of mobile phones. Already, mobiles have been used by schoolchildren for a number of nefarious purposes, such as bullying and victimisation (BBC News 2000), cheating (BBC News 2006), and invasion of privacy (*Khaleej Times* 2004), prompting a number of authorities to introduce a range of rules and protocols for the acceptable use of mobile technologies in education.

In many schools, mobile phones with cameras are prohibited or restricted for the very reasons listed above. More than half of all the schools in London have already banned them completely (*Evening Standard* 2005), principally because of their nuisance value. Children, therefore, use them predominantly as an informal educational tool or, more likely, as a means to communicate with friends and family outside of school life. Despite the problems they bring, mobile technologies have the potential to offer huge benefits in formal education settings. It is time to turn the mobile telephone to effective use through a creative reconceptualisation of pedagogy.

Mobile technologies in education

As with any new technology, mobile wireless devices have already been pressed into limited service as educational tools. So-called 'handheld learning' is slowly gaining in popularity in schools, colleges and universities, and research is now being conducted into its effectiveness. For the early adopters, the implementation of mobile technology has already been successful.

In one example, interactive learning technology-based resources for basic skills were created to encourage the use of ICT by both staff and learners in community education. Educational materials were sent to handheld devices to increase learning access in the community, especially in locations not equipped with computers (Thomas Danby College 2004). Consider the applications of this for home–school linking – a few minor changes would be all that is required to adapt this approach to National Curriculum delivery.

In another example, a mobile learning (m-learning) project conducted in the UK, Italy and Sweden in 2005 focused on 250 young people between the ages of sixteen and twenty-four who had dropped out of school and were unemployed, homeless or travellers. The project used mobile phones and PDAs to provide them with learning materials, access to the Internet and collaborative learning activities. The project helped to improve young people's confidence, increased their levels of concentration and raised their levels of literacy and numeracy skills, proffering them a better chance of employment. The programme manager, Jill Attewell, reported:

> There are many different ways of learning. The traditional classroom doesn't suit everyone. What we set out to discover was whether we could use young people's interest in, and enthusiasm for, mobile technologies to engage them in learning. The findings were very positive. It's clear that mobile phones and PDAs have enormous potential as learning tools – and we now have pocket sized computers with the ability to deliver learning and provide access to online systems and services that are very sophisticated. Although the aim was to find out whether this mode of learning worked with the disengaged, it clearly has huge potential for others as well.
>
> (http://www.publictechnology.net)

Implications for home and school learning

It is clear that the mobile telephone is one of the technology success stories of this new century and that it offers great potential to strengthen links between school and community. The mobile phenomenon raises several important implications for schooling in the coming years. Strengthening the links between school and home provides many benefits for young people and schools alike. Electronic homogeneous workspaces which are location independent, coupled with instantaneous communication and flexible access to digital resources when and where they are required are all obvious advantages. Increased parental involvement with a child's learning is also a clear benefit, as is the ability of schools to provide up-to-date and regular information to parents at the touch of a key.

Collaborative learning activities help students to engage at many levels in problem-solving, decision-making and participation in a community of learning, yielding many positive outcomes, including the development and sharpening of transferable life skills. Most of this can be achieved without the use of ICT, but, with it, the opportunities are increased, as resources are infinitely more accessible. However, for them to be used successfully, there is still the barrier of acceptance to overcome – many schools have banned the use of mobile phones. Until the benefits are perceived to outweigh the threats, this is likely to remain the case.

Conclusion

Schools are changing beyond recognition from the days of chalkboards and rows of desks. One of the driving factors of school innovation is the proliferation of ICT in all its various guises, which are beginning to extend learning beyond the walls of the traditional classroom. Perhaps the most radical change in school education has yet to be achieved. This will be the ultimate blending of boundaries between school and home – a space in which the learner can develop flexibly and in a manner which is time and location independent. It is a space in which dynamic partnerships can flourish between community and school, and between teachers, children and parents, and in which the freedom to explore, create and communicate becomes less limited and more focused. When used appropriately and thoughtfully, digital technologies and mobile devices will be the key to unlocking this alternative future for education.

11 Continuing professional development

Chapter overview

The lifelong learning agenda is gaining ground. Once, 'just in case' learning was practised across all curricula and had an end point. Now, 'just in time' learning is expedient, and there is no termination date. For teachers, it is vitally important to 'keep apace' of all developments that impact upon professional practice, and we argue here that digital technology has a particularly powerful role to play in supporting this objective. In this chapter, we discuss:

- the professional development implications that might accrue from the increased use of ICT in classroom communities;
- the pedagogical issues that arise when ICT is incorporated into subject and curriculum areas;
- the relationship between research evidence in ICT and teachers' practical professional knowledge.

Introduction

This chapter focuses on a number of issues that have arisen within and across the previous chapters and draws out some of the implications for continuing professional development. Much of the research literature dealing with technology and pedagogy attests to the powerful impact ICT can have on the teaching and learning process. In terms of generic learning, the research indicates that levels of collaboration and communication are enhanced by the use of computers, as are knowledge-building and thinking skills (Sandholz *et al.* 1996, Howe *et al.* 1996, Light *et al.* 1996, Knight and Knight 1995, McFarlane 1997).

In various subject areas, there is also evidence that new technologies afford a range of opportunities that can transform teaching and offer improved possibilities for learning (Vaughan 1997, Barton 1997, Selinger 1998, Haydn 1998, Wheeler 2005). It has also been claimed that using technology well in classrooms can even enable teachers to achieve greater success in helping students to be more effective citizens. While there may be some questions surrounding the methodology of these studies as well as some *ex parti* extrapolation, it is certainly true to say that incorporating ICT into classroom situations can and does alter the traditional balance between teacher and learner. Whether this effect is ultimately 'good' or 'better', however defined, still depends on a host of variables, in particular, the way in which ICT interacts with teachers' personal theories of teaching and their classroom practice.

Some theoretical perspectives

In their analysis of the contribution new technologies can make to teaching and learning, Gregoire *et al.* (1996) provided the following with respect to student learning:

- New technologies can stimulate the development of intellectual skills.
- New technologies can contribute to the ways of learning knowledge, skills and attitudes, although this is dependent on previously acquired knowledge and the type of learning activity.
- New technologies spur spontaneous interest more than traditional approaches.
- Students using new technologies concentrate more than students in traditional settings.

These positive images are, however, balanced by their two further observations of genuine significance:

- The benefit to students of using new technologies is greatly dependent, at least for the moment, on the technological skill of the teacher and the teacher's attitude to the presence of the technology in teaching.
- The skill and this attitude in turn are largely dependent on the training staff have received in this area.

Despite the optimistic inferences behind many of the statements, Gregoire *et al.* (1996) are sounding a warning that technology in itself is not a panacea and that without skilled application by the teachers its benefits may quickly recede. The crucial element remains the way in which new technology is incorporated into pedagogical patterns, and this is in turn dependent upon the impact it has on the personal theories and practices of the teachers deploying new technology in their classrooms. A number of educational reformers have argued that for teachers to be successful in constructing new roles for themselves, they need to open up these theories to scrutiny by coming together in discourse communities where various types of knowledge and expertise are shared in rich conversations about practice. These communities then serve to challenge patterns of classroom teaching and learning that have historically been resistant to change.

This 'folk pedagogy', as Bruner (1996) terms it, evolves from the integration of a species-specific theory of mind and a culturally well-established 'folk psychology'. Seen as a whole, 'folk pedagogy' constitutes a set of beliefs about knowledge, learning, thinking, motivation, the 'self' and other psychological and pedagogic categories. It is often intuitive, tacit and sometimes derivative and, in terms of school teaching, is usually embedded within an established subject sub-culture which is itself reinforced by generations of practice. From a socio-cultural perspective, critics have claimed that too often the existing cultures in schools and traditional 'applied' professional development programmes do not always value or support critical and reflective explorations of teaching and learning which are a necessary condition for change. Ball (1994: 16) has characterised many of the discussions in professional-development activities as mere 'style shows' that provide few opportunities for meaningful reflection and growth. And, as a result, teaching remains: 'a *smorgasbord* of alternatives with no real sense of community, there is no basis for comparing or choosing from among alternatives, no basis for real and helpful debate. This lack impedes the capacity to grow.'

Several recent developments have tried to counteract this process. The Community of Learning project (Wineburg and Grossman 1998), for instance, brought together teachers of history and English with university-based educators to read and discuss key texts, to analyse practice and to design lessons that challenged traditional norms. All brought different forms of knowledge with them, and none was privileged. As a result, entrenched ideas were challenged, and new ideas were embraced that had a direct impact on classroom practice. Similarly, Davis and Sumara (1997) described the development of a year-long community of practice that enabled the participating teachers to appreciate how their practice was influenced by prevailing conceptions of teaching and learning even as they were attempting to reconceptualise their practice. A final exemplar comes from the work of Westheimer and Kahne (1993: 326), who argue that if teachers are to foster community-building in their own classroom contexts, they must experience 'opportunities for inter-action, mutual dependence, and identification with a group'.

A crucial component of professional growth is, therefore, the germination and sustaining of groups of individuals in what we have termed 'subject' or 'curriculum' communities. They need to come together in pursuit of a shared experience, one that will both challenge and enhance their practice beyond the life of the project. Of crucial significance are the range of discussions concerning the social nature of knowledge and the interdependence of social and individual processes in the 'co-construction' of that knowledge (John-Steiner and Mahn, 1996). We are of the belief that if thought, learning and the construction of knowledge are not just influenced by social factors but are, in fact, social phenomena (Rogoff 1994), then it makes sense to provide occasions for interaction, joint deliberation and the collective pursuit of shared goals. Only then will teachers be able to make the necessary reflective transfer (Schon 1988) that will enable them to incorporate such ideas into their practice.

Principles of professional development

We therefore suggest that three principles should underpin any professional-development process. First, there should be a focus on pedagogical content knowledge. Grossman (1990) describes this as an overarching conception of how to teach a particular subject. It can be thought of as a conceptual map that guides pedagogical decision-making, both in the planning and interactive phases of teaching. We hold that a teacher's orientation reflects a set of knowledge and beliefs regarding a particular epistemology that belongs to a family – a subject sub-culture with traditions and antecedents. When attempts are made to develop new or innovative practices, this orientation often forms an intuitive screen through which professional development and the teaching reforms are interpreted. Research in several subject areas has demonstrated that teachers only tend to adopt new practices if the assump-tions inherent in the innovation are consistent with their epistemological beliefs and personal theories.

In terms of the use of ICT, Dwyer *et al.* (1994) and Yocum (1996) found that teachers with a more constructivist orientation were more likely to select open-ended software than their more behaviourist colleagues. Similarly, Maor and Taylor (1995) found that the ways in which teachers used new technology varied according to their epistemological orientation. Furthermore, Gobbo and Girardi (2002), in a study of the relationship between teachers' beliefs and the integration of ICT in Italian schools, found that both personal theories of teaching and levels of competence did influence utilisation levels as well as modalities of use. These tended to run parallel to the pedagogical style and episte-mological views espoused by the teachers. Finally, Dwyer and his colleagues (1991) conclude that even where teachers were dedicated to the investigation of the potential of technology to enhance learning, they were often held in check by personal and institutional habits and by variations in the provision of equipment and appropriate classroom structures. Bearing this literature in mind, we see ICT use not as an end in itself but as a catalyst to spur on a shift from transmissionist forms of pedagogy to more social-constructivist approaches. We will return to this issue of orientation later when describing some of the ways in which individual teachers and teams have confronted this aspect of their work and moved to new positions.

Second, there needs to be an emphasis on classroom as a community. This builds on Woolgar's (1988) idea of scientific discovery occurring at the 'workbench'. Workbench communities typically involve small groups of individuals who work closely together in ongoing collaboration to solve problems of immediate and joint concern. Woolgar (1988) points out that at this fundamental level, science looks very much like problem-solving in other domains. He argues, however, that their work is fundamentally dependent on the principles and acceptance of the wider professional community of scientists. The workbench scientists, therefore, have to set their work within this larger context and show publicly that they have met accepted expectations. An analogous 'classroom community' would, therefore, be characterised by small collaborative groups – teachers, teacher educators and researchers, perhaps – who mutually support the growth of the community throughout its lifespan. The community members would be highly interactive and interdependent, working together to use and evaluate the tools at their disposal (material and intellectual), both from their own and from the wider community.

Third, prominence must be placed on intellectual activity. Following Lave and Wenger (1991, 1998) and Rogoff (1994), any professional-development activity must try to transform the understandings, roles and responsibilities of community members. To understand what this means in terms of professional development, it is important to conceptualise teaching as an intellectual activity involving complex judgements and decision-making, where knowledge is utilised from a number of domains. Activities must, therefore, be predicated on the belief that the intellectual activities of planning, enacting and reflecting upon one's teaching are central to professional learning, and that these processes are iterative and longitudinal. One of the guiding lights is, therefore, not only the levels of change observed within each teacher's practice but also the sorts of transformations that take place in each teacher's classroom culture. This will, of course, impact on the most important element, that is, improved student learning.

The three perspectives are shaped by the idea that neither top-down nor bottom-up forms of professional development are sufficient to bring about the creative use of new technologies in classrooms. The former suggests a model in which knowledge and practice are transferred by experts to novices, while the latter suggests a model in which one is left to discover knowledge by oneself or with peers (Rogoff 1994). Whilst accepting that professional learning can occur in both these settings, it is our contention that neither will lead to sustained changes in practice.

Teaching about or teaching through ICT

The first issue relates to what Selinger (2002) has called the tension between teaching about ICT and teaching through ICT. Many of the chapters illustrate the importance of changing the classroom context as a prerequisite to enhanced ICT use (see Chapter 5). This is seen as particularly important if greater collaborative work is to be fostered. Also, if the ultimate goal is to make the digital tool support and enhance learning, then students have to be enabled to make the tool work for them (Selinger 2002). However, teachers need to be aware of cognitive overload where, according to Chandler (1995), repetitive visual text and accompanying auditory support might impose an extraneous cognitive load. The dangers are highlighted by Hoyles *et al.* (1994), who argue that collaborative work around ICT needs careful preparation and skilled support. Most importantly, tasks need to lend themselves to group work and the software should be appropriate and the hardware sufficient for the task. The importance of 'scaffolding the task' with support materials that focus on the process of exploration, therefore emphasises the salience of 'a framework of structured independence together with pupil autonomy' (Hoyles *et al.* 1994: 214). Such processes need to be at the heart of any professional-development activity.

The importance of pedagogical style

This leads on to a second issue, namely, the importance and continuation of a strong teacher role. This is inevitably connected to the epistemological orientations and personal theories of each teacher; however, such roles connect with established school subject sub-cultures to create a particular 'pedagogical style'. This is an amorphous concept and can encompass several dimensions, but of crucial importance is the fact that variations of style will be influenced by the pervasive subject sub-culture which has become embedded within the department or faculty in which the teacher is located. This juxtaposition of personal style and subject cultural factors is an interesting one given the prominence (and scarcity) of ICT within certain subject areas. It can also be problematic for some subjects in that the use of ICT is predicated on the idea of collaborative or more individualised learning. This is augmented by the idea that new technology conveys implicitly to children that they can work at their own pace. However, established teaching styles are often based on synchronicity, while the curriculum demands a sequencing of content so that students can be 'moved' through at a particular speed. This accords with Selinger's view (2002) that expertise with the technology must be balanced with the subject learning. Also, as many of the presentations indicate, if handled well, ICT can increase levels of motivation, particularly amongst the apparently 'least able'.

It seems that subject teachers do not wish to surrender to the technology but prefer to integrate it into their established subject and personal pedagogical style. In particular, they do not want to replace subject learning with technical training. This is due to the fact that subjects carry with them certain assumptions about 'knowledge', 'worthwhile learning', the 'good student', 'effective practice', and what constitutes 'acceptable performance' (Goodson and Mangen 1995).

In some subject areas, for instance, mathematics and science (where the take-up of ICT has been more widespread), enthusiasm may be more obvious, perhaps because its use fits more snugly with existing practice. In contrast, teachers in other subjects – history, geography and English, for example – may feel they have to modify the use of ICT in order to ensure that it does not disrupt their established patterns of teaching or their place in the curriculum. This process of adjustment and accommodation will be an essential prerequisite to any professional-development programme. In many ways, this adjustment within an established pattern is the way in which teachers have reacted to both educational reforms and to the introduction of technologies throughout the history of schooling.

Competence and confidence

In many schools, digital tools will inevitably be used pragmatically and become another resource – albeit a powerful one – amongst many. It is also clear that each teacher's orientation and personal theories of learning and teaching will influence the model of teaching and learning adopted, although the research shows the greater the confidence in the technology the greater the propensity for use. This motivation factor is vital to the success of the project and beyond. In fact, it is part of a loop of professional learning that incorporates a number of variables, including competence, theories of teaching, subject perceptions and knowledge, as well as levels of professional satisfaction. It is, therefore, posited that once improved learning outcomes or increased classroom interaction and motivation become noticed, so the teacher's level of confidence will improve and the variables will re-enter the loop adjusted in a more favourable position. This is the iterative process that will inevitably form the core of any professional-development process or programme.

Activity

Cox et al. (2000) take this further and highlight both the positive and negative factors that can influence the deployment and use of ICT. Using the categories below, discuss or define the relative value of using ICT and provide evidence from your own professional practice.

Table 11.1 The positive and negative factors in the deployment of ICT

Positive factors	*Negative factors*
Makes my lessons more interesting	Makes my lessons more difficult
Makes my lessons more diverse	Makes my lessons less fun
Has improved the presentation of materials for my lessons	Reduces pupils' motivation
Gives me more prestige	Impairs pupils' learning
Makes my administration more efficient	Restricts the content of the lessons
Gives me more confidence	Is not enjoyable
Makes the lessons more fun	Takes up too much time
Enhances my career prospects	Is counter-productive due to insufficient technical resources
Helps me to discuss teaching ideas	

Source: Adapted from Cox *et al.* (2002).

Conclusion

Some feared that the introduction of new technologies into classrooms would result in a heightened sense of social efficiency where a mix of systems, instructional packages and various forms of technological wizardry would create its own technical fix to the perceived problems of education. Hartley (1998), for instance, warns against the hidden curriculum of new technology where policy-makers can mandate practice from above through the seemingly value-neutral technology. The evidence also suggests that there are multiple pedagogical possibilities inherent in technology-based teaching and learning. However, the success or otherwise of such innovations rests on the teacher's ability to recognise that learners develop their own preferred style, and this can be harnessed through a mediated, technology-rich environment.

Such observations imply that if changes in teaching and learning are to be fundamental and long-lasting, then a different model of professional development is needed. At the moment, we have too much 'innovation stretch' where the gap between pioneers and the medium and non-user is wide. For this 'long tail' to be shortened, new and innovative forms of professional development need to be instigated. Currently, most of the professional development to date has been based on the idea of 'retooling', that is, it has been structured to augment the existing curriculum by providing specific training to groups of teachers in the mechanics of the technology. What is needed is that which Watson *et al.* (1999) call a 're-forming' approach whereby training is built on a staged process through which teachers have to pass in order to change their practice. Taylor (1998) identifies these stages as the orientation phase, the adaptation phase, the evaluation phase, the innovation phase and the institutionalisation phase. At present, many of the teachers in 'classroom communities' have moved through the first four phases, albeit at different speeds and levels of complexity.

Of central importance, of course, is the need to persuade school-management teams, LEAs and policy-makers at local and national level that it is not only provision of equipment and its use that matters. The presence of technology alone will not improve practice or education. But technology integrated effectively into learning environments by reflective and flexible educators will help in the restructuring of classrooms and schools (Watson 2002) and ultimately in the transformation of educational provision (Wheeler 2005).

The role of researchers and consultants is vital in this process. They should not be seen as 'providers' of skills and abilities but as reformers and people who can provide leadership and direction to school-based 'change agents'. This, as some of the presentations have shown, can be brought about through increased communication and mutual 'scaffolding' between and among team members. In general, most of the teachers in the subject initiatives reported an increased sense of professionalism (Hoyle and John 1995) and a greater feeling of self-efficacy after working collaboratively. Finally, when dispersing our ideas and practices, it is important that teachers should engage directly in the process of learning that is being offered to the students. This will help teachers get on the inside of the innovation as well as increasing their confidence, competence, experience and understanding of the software and its pedagogical implications. This form of 'authentic' professional development is vital if ICT use is to move beyond mere novelty.

Dwyer *et al.* (1990b) claim that new forms of teaching and learning will result from greater familiarity, confidence and flexibility, and that success is attendant upon increased and long-term use of new technology. As we have shown, in some classrooms, there is indeed a genuine shift taking place from seeing technology less as a patient tutor and more as a tool that can facilitate inquiry and critical thinking. However, in so doing, teachers have to accept that learning in such an environment is often chaotic, messy, may have no tangible beginnings and ends and may breed more confusion before genuine understanding occurs.

12 Harnessing the power of technology

Chapter overview

In this final chapter, we present a metaperspective of the themes and issues that are most likely to impact upon successful deployment of digital technology in education. As you read through it, you should be able to:

- revisit themes related to digital learning technology use;
- consider the implications of technology deployment;
- contextualise these themes within your own professional practice.

Metaphorically speaking . . .

This book has dwelt on the possibilities and practicalities of using digital technologies to enhance the quality of teaching and learning. In the title of this chapter, we have drawn upon the metaphor of 'harnessing power'. We hope the title generates an evocative image of a team of horses drawing a carriage, with each animal working concertedly with the carriage driver, travelling towards a common goal or destination. In a similar manner, teachers can harness the power of technology and work towards the goal of transformative education using some powerful drivers. By using the term 'harnessing', however, we did not intend merely to conjure up convenient images of the relationship between teachers and technology. We also intended that it should convey a sense of the momentum of change and to encapsulate the debate about whether education is being driven by, or is driving, technology towards educational transformation.

We could extend the metaphor further and ask to what extent the carriage driver is in control and what skills he or she requires, or whether he or she is merely 'holding onto the reins'. Many teachers find themselves in this equivocal position when they first encounter a new technology. We might also debate the nature of school-based ICT as either a policy- or needs-driven phenomenon. Ultimately, our metaphor can serve as a useful device to illustrate the daunting task set before every teacher – to prepare a generation of future workers for a world of work that does not yet exist, and one which the teachers themselves might find quite alien even if they were actually able to conceptualise it. So, is education careening down an uncharted path? If so, is technology a part of the problem or a part of the solution? This is, of course, open to debate. Whatever your view, we hope you will agree that the future of education requires successful teamwork, where all elements, including the stakeholders themselves, are harnessing the power of digital technology and driving together in the same direction, towards a common destination.

We have argued that to effectively harness the power of technology so that it can actually enhance and transform the learning experience, major stakeholders must apprehend something of the interplay that exists between learners, teachers, technology and the curriculum. As we have attempted to illustrate throughout this book, this is a far from easy prospect. Such interplay is not only complex and with many layers, it also plays out in what Schön (1987) has called the 'swamp' – the often murky and messy scenarios of everyday teaching and learning, in which little can be quantified and where much is unpredictable. In such circumstances, there are often no written rules or guidelines, and the professional practitioner must 'play it by ear'. We must, therefore, conclude then, that there is a greater need than ever for reflective and intuitive practitioners within the teaching profession.

Further, for this complex interplay to be better understood, effort is required not only on the part of the innovators and early adopters but also by the more reluctant teachers and managers to integrate digital technologies into the 'classroom' and also into the curriculum and, indeed, right into the very heart of the culture of education. This will occur successfully when the pragmatic late majority are convinced of the efficacy and validity of the technology and its applicability to teaching and learning. We have already suggested that the presence of technology in the classroom will not in itself improve educational practice. When professional practitioners engage with technology in a flexible and reflective manner, however, we may then begin to witness substantive progress.

Evidence for the efficacy of digital technology is all around – it now needs to be implemented within the school culture. If traditional learning spaces are to advance from mere 'classrooms' to become 'digital classrooms', the technology must stop being exciting and daunting and become mundane – it must eventually become just another part of the fabric of day-to-day business in the life of the school. In other words, as has been exemplified in Wenger's notion of cultural transparency (1990), and in Norman's (1999) conceptualisation, the computer must become 'invisible' or, at the very least, 'transparent' for users and recipients. After all, learning technology is primarily about learning.

Mind the gap

Psychologically, the gap is inexorably widening between the 'digital natives', the 'digital immigrants' and the 'analogues'. Digital natives have been characterised as the ICT 'whizz kids' or the 'digital generation'. They are generally younger people who have been born and raised in the digital age, and they find themselves infinitely more comfortable using ICT than their parents and, in many cases, their teachers. By contrast, digital immigrants are engaged in 'learning the language' because they are older and were born and raised prior to the digital age, when classrooms contained either primitive computers or none. Many have immersed themselves within digital culture and can talk the new language 'fluently', but their old 'accent' remains. Digital immigrants wish to learn how to use ICT effectively, but for them the new technologies are often opaque and require a great deal of time investment. They are fixed within a print-based 'literacy' model of communication, whereas digital natives are comfortable living in an age where digital communication is dominant. A third category, 'the analogues' tend to either dismiss digital technologies or reluctantly adopt them and struggle to learn how to use them, because for most of their lives they have managed comfortably without them.

Interestingly, for the first time, all three categories are represented within the current teaching profession, spanning as it does a wide age range. Analogues may have a video-cassette recorder at home that has a clock fixed and flashing on '12:00' since the day it was purchased and which they have never learned to programme. Digital immigrants may have bought the latest DVD recorder so that they can watch their favourite movies at home whenever they wish. By contrast, the digital natives are actually creating and editing their own movies using the latest iMac software and then publishing their work for the world to see on YouTube. What will be the teaching methods each will employ with the same group of students? Experiences will differ for the group depending on their teachers' outlooks on technology.

A similar dichotomy can be seen between the 'Baby Boomers' (those born immediately post-Second World War), and the 'Generation Xers' – which, in this volume, we characterise as those born between the mid-1960s and 1980s. Table 12.1 shows the contrasting psycho-social profiles of the two sets of technology users.

From Table 12.1, it should be apparent that the differences between the two groups extend past the use of technology into a number of learning and life-skill related areas. Generation Xers – a generation that have only been in the world of work for a short while – seem to be infinitely better prepared, both mentally and socially, to survive and flourish in a technologically dominated and ever-changing world. The generation immediately following them, referred to as 'Generation Y' (those born between mid-1980s and the turn of the millennium) are even better equipped. They have never known a time devoid of computers, and they have witnessed the aftermath of technological impact upon the Western world to the extent that they take for granted the multifarious uses and influences it has on their lives.

Secondary orality and teacher control

To fully comprehend the tensions being wrought in education through the introduction of new digital technology, we must first understand the development of educational traditions through the centuries. Technologies have driven teaching methods, as teachers draw upon the most appropriate means for each generation's societal needs. Throughout the time prior to the industrial age, teaching was conducted almost exclusively within the oral tradition, and on a one-to-one basis. The population was predominantly illiterate, with

Table 12.1 Contrasting technology user profiles

	Baby Boomers	**Generation Xers**
Independence	Dependent on teacher to define and support learning	Independent problem-solvers and self-starters
Technology	The computer is 'nice to have'	Technology is a 'must have'
Stimulation	Slower pace: it's OK to wait. Gaming is not a serious occupation	Crave stimulation, expect immediate answers and feedback
Relevance	Learn 'what' or 'how' first, then find out 'why'	What's in it for me?
Lifelong learning	Work in the same organisation for life	View job environments as places to grow; have portfolio careers
Learner control	Teacher focus expected	Learner wants more autonomy
Comfort with unknown	Discomfort is avoided	Xers are fearless, hand-holding is not expected

Source: Adapted from DiPaulo (2006).

reading and writing the preserve of the clergy and elite, and the oral tradition was the sole means of knowledge transmission. The industrial age was accompanied by the apprenticeship model of learning, in which orality continued to operate, but now synchronised on a one-to-many basis (the lecture and demonstration). The introduction of print technology prompted a shift in pedagogical emphasis and, ultimately, a challenge to the oral tradition. Over time, the literacy model supplanted much of the oral tradition and continues to dominate educational practices to this day (Ferris and Wilder 2006).

However, it is only since the introduction of the digital technologies, and in particular hypertext and mobile telephony, that electronic literacy has begun to influence practice. This new literacy, or 'secondary orality' (Ong 1982) has ushered in a previously unknown freedom for learners to explore and construct their own knowledge, outside of and beyond the influence of their teachers. This can be witnessed in the unstructured activities of wikis and blogs, multidirectional and casual 'surfing' of the web and, most markedly, in the chaotic morass of quasi-literate text-messaging.

Yet, as we have previously argued, many teachers blissfully continue to practise within the old model of literacy, futilely attempting to maintain their authority and ownership of knowledge through control of text-based knowledge (Ferris and Wilder 2006). We refer here not to teachers' reluctance to depart from transmission models of teaching but rather to their dependence upon practices rooted in textuality. Digital technology has already impacted deeply upon education, ostensibly ensuring that control has passed to the learners and that the traditional instructor role has begun to irrevocably change. As a part of the move toward the digital classroom, teachers now need to acknowledge, no matter how uncomfortably, that it is time to relinquish at least some or their control and move towards a secondary orality model of teaching. This will permit new courses to be 'future proofed' and designed in a manner that is culturally relevant to the digital natives.

Digital literacy

The second part of the digital-classroom equation is the level and nature of skill necessary for learners to maximise their use of technology. There is a need, for example, for students to engage with digital media in a number of ways, transcending those which are required to learn from paper-based text or images. For example, learning from digital media requires that students not only read and think but also point and click (Tapscott 1998). Digital literacy could, thus, be described as a convergence of cognitive and psychomotor skills exemplified in hand–eye coordination. Oseas and Wood (2003) go further, arguing that students now need to possess *multiple* literacy skills to gain access to all the benefits digital media offer. Knowing how to download, store and retrieve learning objects in a number of different formats or how to 'read a photograph' – known as visual literacy – are just some of the new skills students will need to acquire to be successful learners.

Education on the move

Within this book, we have explored the potential of digital technologies to extend the school beyond its traditional boundaries, both physically and philosophically. The use of a number of Internet-based utilities can strongly stamp a school's virtual presence, whilst the use of e-mail can raise the actual profile of the school within the home, strengthening links between the two. It is the mobile technologies, however, that seem to present the most distinct possibilities for learning beyond traditional boundaries and constraints.

Today's youth is constantly on the move, travelling further and more frequently, constantly seeking new experiences and spending less time rooted to one job than did their elders. They are engaged in 'portfolio careers' in which regular changes of career are not only inevitable but perhaps also expedient for the economic health of the nation. They see change as an opportunity to learn and adapt, and never as a threat. Mobile technologies are a 'must-have' for this generation, and, at present, they provide the best solution for lifelong learning on the move.

Digital technologies are revolutionising the manner in which education is conducted, from curriculum design and resource development through to assessment of learning and record-keeping. Teaching methods are gradually changing too, despite resistance, due in no small part to the introduction of interactive and personal technologies into the traditional learning space. Outside of the classroom, social technologies such as wikis and blogs are providing the impetus for expert communities of practice to evolve, emerge and connect together, and this movement is set to become even more influential. The emerging digital video-clip repositories such as YouTube will provide further impetus for the production and wide dissemination of creative communication. Most strikingly, young people will take an active role in the future development of all of these technologies. Mobile-communication devices are transforming the language children use in a creative if somewhat disconcerting manner through short message service (SMS) texting. The onus is now on teachers to attempt to exploit these technologies to promote new forms of interactive learning.

Access all areas

Access to learning resources is now at an unprecedented scale, courtesy of the ever-expanding World Wide Web. Although at the time of writing it is only fifteen years old, in its present incarnation the Internet has opened up a raft of new possibilities to transform the school experience. If we are to believe the likes of Jimmy Wales of Wikipedia who asks us to 'Imagine a world in which every single person is given free access to the sum of all human knowledge. That's what we're doing', then we must acknowledge that the resources already exist and that they will continue to proliferate. Much of what exists in physical format has already been transferred onto digital format and sits somewhere on the web waiting to be found and used. Schools that do not exploit digital resources will be in danger of falling behind in the race to prepare lifelong learners who are able to live and work in a world of constant change.

We have already seen that the role of the teacher is changing. The only part of the equation to be put into place is the role the teacher should play in the filtering, organisation and facilitation of these vast digital repositories of knowledge so that students can learn in new and creative ways. As we have already indicated, we believe that the school ICT coordinator will play a crucial role in this process. Timely in-service training, expert 'best practice' modelling and action research will all yield dividends.

Creative approaches to teaching have been encouraged through the use of digital devices such as cameras, digital recording and programmable devices, leading to an entirely new range of learning experiences across all of the key stages. For the first time, students are in a position to be able to create their own personalised, individually tailored learning resources, to become their own publishers and to run their own recording studios, all from a common, ubiquitous platform. Teachers have an important role to play in this process as facilitators, rather than instructors.

Into the unknown

The use of digital technology in schools is preparing learners to enter a rapidly changing world of work in which business and industry are conducted at break-neck speed and in which a bewildering array of new technologies is exerting an influence. It has been predicted that the majority of new jobs created in the next few years will be based predominantly or exclusively on the use of the computer (Molyneaux 2003). Children are acquiring a range of transferable skills previously unavailable to their parents, and they will certainly need them to survive in a computer-dominated society. Although this generational chasm could be viewed as divisive, teachers must optimistically view the use of digital technologies as more than just a means to an end and instead view them as a range of mind tools that will encourage a new generation of learners to think critically, independently and creatively. It is only with these transferable life skills that children can be prepared for a world of work that does not yet exist, and one which teachers find impossible to describe.

None of us can predict what the world will look like in the future, but one thing is certain: technology will play a major role in its shaping. We can also be certain that those who learn how to harness technology effectively will be the best prepared to meet its challenges.

Bibliography

Albaugh, P. (1997) *The Role of Skepticism in Preparing Teachers for the Use of Technology* (ERIC Document Reproduction Services, ED 406 339).

Andrews, R. (2000) 'Framing and Design in ICT in English: Towards a New Subject and Practices in the Classroom', in A. Goodwyn (ed.), *English in the Digital Age: Information and Communications Technology and the Teaching of English*, London: RoutledgeFalmer, pp. 22–3.

Argyris, C. and Schön, D. (1974) *Theory in Practice: Increasing Professional Effectiveness*, San Francisco, Calif.: Jossey-Bass.

Armstrong, V., Barnes, S., Sutherland, R., Curran, S., Mills, S. and Thompson, I. (2005) 'Collaborative Research Methodology for Investigating Teaching and Learning: The Use of Interactive Whiteboard Technology', *Educational Review*, 57 (4): 457–69.

Audit Commission (2006) 'Special Educational Needs: A Mainstream Issue', available online at http://www.auditcommission.gov.uk/reports/national-report.asp?categoryid=andprodid=d3265d20-fd7d-11d6-b211-0060085f8572andsectionid=sect5 (accessed 11 July 2006).

Baggott La Velle, L. B., Mcfarlane, A. and Brawn, R. (2003a) 'Knowledge Transformation through ICT in Science Education: A Case Study in Teacher-Driven Curriculum Development – Case Study 1', *British Journal of Educational Technology*, 34 (2): 183–99.

Baggott La Velle, L. B., Mcfarlane, A., John, P. D. and Brawn, R. (2003b) 'According to the Promises: The Subculture of School Science, Teachers' Pedagogical Identity and the Challenge of ICT', *Education, Communication and Information*, 4 (1): 109–29.

Ball, D. L. (1994) 'Developing Mathematics Reform: What We Don't Know About Teaching and Learning but Would Make Good Working Hypotheses', paper presented at the Conference on Teacher Education in Mathematics, Arlington, Va.

Ball, B. (2003) 'Teaching and Learning Mathematics with an Interactive Whiteboard', *Micromath*, 19 (1).

Ball, S. (1981) *Beachside Comprehensive: A Case Study of Secondary Schooling*, Cambridge: Cambridge University Press.

—— and Lacey, A. (1984) 'Subject Disciplines as the Opportunity for Group Action: A Measured Critique of Subject Sub-Cultures', in A. Hargreaves and P. Woods (eds), *Classrooms and Staffrooms*, Milton Keynes: Open University Press, pp. 234–44.

Barnes, D. (1976) *From Communication to Curriculum*, Harmondsworth: Penguin.

Barnett, M. (1994) 'Designing the Future? Technology Values and Choice', *International Journal of Technology and Design Education*, 4 (3): 51–64.

Barton, R. (1997) 'Does Data Logging Change the Nature of Children's Thinking in Experimental Work in Science', in N. Davis and B. Somekh (eds), *Using IT Effectively in Teaching and Learning*, London: Routledge, pp. 63–72.

Bassey, M. (1999) *Case Study Research in Educational Settings*, Milton Keynes: Open University Press.

Baudrillard, J. (1996) *The Consumer Society: Myths and Structures*, London: Sage.

BBC News (2000) 'Bullies Use Mobile Phone Threats', available online at http://news.bbc.co.uk/1/hi/education/671681.stm (accessed 19 June 2006).

—— (2005) 'Net-Illiterate "Failing Children"', available online at http://news.bbc.co.uk/1/hi/uk/4490879.stm (accessed 11 July 2006).

—— (2006) 'Mobiles Fuel Exam Cheating Rise', available online at http://news.bbc.co.uk/1/hi/education/4848224.stm (accessed 19 June 2006).

Beard, R. (1999) *National Literacy Strategy: Review of Research and Other Related Evidence*, London: DfEE.

Becta (2001) 'The "Digital Divide": A Discussion Paper', available online at http://www.becta.org.uk/page_documents/research/digitaldivide.pdf (accessed 18 July 2006).

—— (2003) *What Research Says About Interactive Whiteboards*, London: Becta.

—— (2004) *A Review of the Literature on the Barriers to the Up-Take of ICT by Teachers*, London: Becta.

—— (2005) 'Home School Links Mediated through ICT', available online at http://www.becta.org.uk/research/research.cfm?section=1andid=534 (accessed 7 July 2006).

—— (2006) *Transforming Learning and Teaching through ICT*, London: Becta.

Bell, M. A. (2002) 'Why Use an Interactive Whiteboard: A Baker's Dozen Reasons, Teachers', *Net Gazette*, 3 (1), available online at http://teachers.net/gazette/JAN02/mabell.html (accessed 8 November 2007).

Berger, K. S. (1994) *The Developing Person*, New York: Worth Publishers.

Birch, J. (2003) 'Using an electronic whiteboard', available online at http://www.bucksict.org.uk/Teacher%20Resources/DownloadDocs/Curriculum/Whiteboards.doc (accessed 21 November 2007).

Bishop, A. J. (1988) 'Mathematics Education in its Cultural Context', *Educational Studies in Mathematics*, 19 (2): 179–91.

Blair, Tony (1998) 'Foreword to Connecting the Learning Society', consultation paper on the National Grid for Learning.

—— (2004) 'Speech at the Guardian's Public Services Summit', London, 29 January.

Booth, T. and Ainscow, M (2002) *Index for Inclusion: Developing Learning and Participation in Schools*, Bristol: Centre for Studies in Inclusive Education.

Bosley, C. and Moon, S. (2003) *A Review of the Existing Literature on the Use of ICT Within an Educational Context*, Derby: Centre for Guidance Studies, University of Derby.

Boulos, M. N. K., Maramba, I. and Wheeler S. (2006) 'Wikis, Blogs and Podcasts: A New Generation of Web-Based Tools for Virtual Collaborative Clinical Practice and Education', *BMC Medical Education*, 6 (41), available online at http://www.Biomedcentral.com/1472-6920/6/41 (accessed 31 January 2007).

Bristol and Plymouth BARE Programme (2001), available online at http://www.recordingand assessment.co.uk (accessed 17 July 2006).

—— (2006), available online at http://www.recordingandassessment.co.uk/support.htm

Brosnan, M. (1998) *Technophobia: The Psychological Impact of Information Technology*, London: Routledge.

Bruner, J. S. (1986) *Actual Minds, Possible Worlds*, Cambridge, Mass.: Harvard University Press.

—— (1996) *The Culture of Education*, Cambridge, Mass.: Harvard University Press.

Butle, D. and Sellbom, M. (2002) 'Barriers to Adopting Technology for Teaching and Learning', *Educase Quarterly* 25 (2): 22–8.

Castells, M. (1997) *End of Millennium: The Information Age: Economy, Society and Culture*, Cambridge, Mass.: Blackwell.

Centre for Studies in Inclusive Education (2002), available online at http://inclusion.uwe.ac.uk/csie (accessed 5 June 2007).

Chandler, P. (1995) 'Is Conventional Computer Instruction Ineffective for Learning?', paper presented at the Australian Computers in Education Conference, Perth, 9–13 January.

Chapelle, C. A. (2001) *Computer Applications in Second Language Acquisition*, Cambridge: Cambridge University Press.

Clarke, Charles (2004) Speech at the National BETT Conference.

Clarke, S. (2005) *Formative Assessment in the Secondary Classroom*, Abingdon: Hodder Murray.

Cope, B. and Kalantzis, M. (2000) *Multiliteracies: Literacy Learning and the Design of Social Futures*, London: Routledge.

Cotton, J. (1995) *The Theory of Assessment: An Introduction*, London: Kogan Page.

Counsell, C. (2003) 'The Forgotten Games Kit: Putting Historical Thinking First in Long-, Medium- and Short-Term Planning', in T. Haydn and C. Counsell (eds), *History, ICT and Learning in the Secondary School*, London: RoutledgeFalmer, pp. 52–108.

Cox, M. J., Preston C. and Cox, K (1999) 'What Factors Support or Prevent Teachers from Using ICT in Their Classrooms?', paper presented at the British Educational Research Association Annual Conference, University of Sussex at Brighton, 2–5 September.

Cuban, L. (1999) 'The Technology Puzzle', *Education Week*, 18 (43).

—— (2001) *Oversold and Underused: Computers in the Classroom*, Cambridge, Mass.: Harvard University Press.

——, Kirkpatrick, H. and Peck, C. (2001) 'High Access and Low Use Technology in High School Classrooms: Explaining the Apparent Paradox American Educational Research', *American Educational Research Journal*, 38 (4): 813–34.

Dale, R., Robertson, S. and Shortis, T. (2004) 'You Can't Not Go with the Technological Flow, Can You?' Constructing "ICT" and "Teaching and Learning"', *Journal of Computer Assisted Learning*, 20(6): 456–70.

Davis, B. and Sumara, D. (1997) 'Cognition, Complexity and Teacher Education', *Harvard Education Review* 67 (1): 105–25.

Davison, J. (2000) 'Literacy and social class', in J. Davison and J. Moss (eds), *Issues in English Teaching*, London: Routledge, pp. 243–59.

Dawes, L. (2000) 'The National Grid for Learning and the Professional Development of Teachers', Ph.D. thesis, De Montford University.

Dawkins, R. (1999) *The Selfish Gene*, Oxford: Oxford University Press.

—— (2003) *A Devil's Chaplain*, London: Weidenfeld and Nicolson.

Design and Technology Association. Available online at http://web.data.org.uk/data/secondary/crosscurr_ict.php (accessed 27 June 2006).

DfEE (1998) *Open for Learning, Open for Business*, DfEE, London, http://www.dfee.gov.uk/grid/challenge/index.htm

—— (2000) *The Use of ICT in Subject Teaching: Expected Outcomes for Teachers in England, Northern Ireland and Wales*, London: TTA.

DfES (1997) 'Connecting the Learning Society: National Grid for Learning', The Government's Consultation Paper, available online at http://www.dfes.gov.uk/consultations/downloadable Docs/42_1.pdf (accessed 8 November 2007).

—— (2001) 'National Curriculum Online. Inclusion: Providing Effective Learning Opportunities for All Pupils', available online at http://www.nc.uk.net/nc_resources/html/inclusion.shtml (accessed 1 May 2006).

—— (2002) *Statistics of Education: The School Workforce in England 2000*, London: TMO.

—— (2005a) 'Cross Government Guidance: Sharing Information on Children and Young People (Education Consultation)', available online at http://www.dfes.gov.uk/consultations/con results.cfm?consultationid=1366 (accessed 11 July 2006).

—— (2005b) 'Higher Standards, Better Schools for All: More Choice for Parents and Pupils' Education White Paper, available online at http://www.dfes.gov.uk/publications/schools whitepaper (accessed 15 July 2006).

—— (2006a) 'National Curriculum Assessments at Key Stage 1 in England', available online at http://www.dfes.gov/rsgateway/DB/SFR/s000672/SFR30-2006.pdf (accessed 8 November 2007).

—— (2006b) 'Personalised Learning: A Flexible Curriculum', available online at http://www.standards.dfes.gov.uk/personalisedlearning (accessed 1 July 2006).

—— (2006c) 'Home School Agreement: Parental Involvement', available online at http://www.Standards. Dfes.gov.uk/Parentalinvolvement/Hsa (accessed 18 July 2006).

—— 'Excellence and Enjoyment: Social and Emotional Aspects of Learning', available online at http://www.bandapilot.org.uk/pages/seal/index.html (accessed 21 July 2006).

Dillenburg, P. and Schneider, D. (1995) 'The Mechanisms of Collaborative Learning', paper presented at ICCAI Conference, Geneva, available online at http://www.tecfa.unige.ch/tecfa/research/cmc/colla/iccai95_5.html (accessed 28 June 2006).

DiPaulo, A. (2006) 'Moving to Anywhere, Anytime Learning', keynote speech to the fifteenth EDEN Conference, Technical University of Vienna, 14–16 June.

Disability Discrimination Act (1995) 'Chapter 50, Part 4: Education', available online at http://www.opsi.gov.uk/acts/acts1995/1995050.htm (accessed 5 June 2006).

Dossiers Pratiques en Technopedagogie Universitaire). Available online at http://www.profetic.org:16080/dossiers/article.php3?id_article=973 (accessed 15 August 2006).

Dwyer, D. C., Ringstaff, C. and Sandholz, J. H. (1990) *Teacher Beliefs and Practices*, Cupertino, Calif.: Apple Computers.

Dyke, J. and Smither, J. (1994) 'Age Differences in Computer Anxiety: The Role of Computer Experience, Gender and Education', *Journal of Educational Computing Research*, 10 (3): 239–48.

EC (14 February 2001) Report from the Education Council to the European Council, 'The concrete future objectives of education and training systems', 5980/01.

E-Learning Foundation (2006). Available online at http://www.e-learningfoundation.com/uploads/what%20the%20research%20says_2.pdf (accessed 20 July 2006).

Eraut, M. (2000) 'Non-Formal Learning, Implicit Learning and Tacit Knowledge in Professional Work', in F. Coffield (ed.), *The Necessity of Informal Learning*, Bristol: Policy Press, pp. 12–31.

—— (2002) 'Menus for Choosy Diners', *Teachers and Teaching, Theory and Practice*, 8 (3), available online at http://www.informaworld.com/smpp/title~content=t713447546~db=all~tab=issueslist~branches=8-v88 (accessed 8 November 2007).

Ertmer, P. (1999) 'Addressing first and second order barriers to change: Strategies for technology implementation', *Educational Technology Research and Development*, 47(4), pp. 47–61.

European Agency (2005) Available online at http://www.european-agency.org/nat_ovs/united_kingdom/4.html (accessed 12 July 2006).

Evening Standard (2005) 'Half of Schools Banning Mobiles', 10 June, available online at http://www.thisislondon.co.uk/news/articles/19218238?source=evening%20standard (accessed 19 July 2006).

Fabry, D. and Higgs, J. (1997) 'Barriers to the Effective Use of Technology in Education', *Journal of Educational Computing*, 17 (4): 385–95.

Fairbrother, B. and Harrison, C. (2001) 'Assessing Pupils' in J. Dillon and M. Maguire (eds), *Becoming a Teacher*, 2nd edn, Buckingham: Open University Press, pp. 182–91.

Feldman, A. (2003) 'Science: Venturing Online to Teach and Learn', in T. Gordon (ed.), *The Digital Classroom*, Cambridge, Mass.: Harvard University Press, pp. 90–102.

Ferris, S. P. and Wilder, H. (2006) 'Uses and Potentials of Wikis in the Classroom', *Innovate*, 2 (5), available online at http://www.innovateonline.info/index.php?view=articleandid=258 (accessed 20 August 2006).

Finlayson, H. M. and Perry, A. (1995) 'Turning Sceptics into Missionaries: The Case for Compulsory Information Technology Courses', *Journal of Information Technology for Teacher Education*, 4 (3): 351–61.

Fit for Purpose. Available online at http://www.yourwindow.to/information-security/gl_fitforpurpose.htm (accessed 20 June 2006).

Fitzpatrick, G. (1998) 'The Locales Framework: Understanding and Designing Co-Operative Work', unpublished Ph.D. thesis, University of Queensland.

Florian, L. (1998) 'An Examination of the Practical Problems Associated with the Implementation of Inclusive Practice', *Support for Learning* 13 (3): 105–8.

—— (2000) 'Inclusive Practice: What, How and Why', in C. Tilstone, L. Florian and R. Rose (eds), *Promoting Inclusive Practice*, London: RoutledgeFalmer, pp. 13–25.

Forman, E. A. and Cazden, C. B. (1986) 'Exploring Vygotskian Perspectives in Education: The Cognitive Value of Peer Interaction', in J. V. Wertsch (ed.), *Culture, Communication and Cognition: Vygotskian Perspectives*, New York: Cambridge University Press, pp. 323–47.

Fox, B. (2003) *Successful ICT Leadership in Primary Schools*, Exeter: Learning Matters.

Futurelab (2005) 'Viewpoint: The Rise and Rise of the Mobile Phone', available online at http://www.futurelab.org.uk/viewpoint/art50.htm (accessed 19 July 2006).

Galton, M., Simon, B. and Croll, P. (1980) *Inside the Primary Classroom*, London: Routledge.

Gamble, N. and Easingwood, N. (eds) (2001) *ICT and Literacy*, London: Continuum.

Giangreco, M. F. (1997) 'Key Lessons Learned about Inclusive Education: Summary of the 1996 Schonell Memorial Lecture', *International Journal of Disability, Development and Education*, 44 (3): 193–206.

Giddens, A. (1984) *The Constitution of Society: Outline of the Theory of Structuration*, Berkeley, Calif.: University of California Press.

Gobbo, C. and Girardi, G. (2002) 'Teachers' Beliefs and the Integration of ICT in Italian Schools', *Journal of Information Technology for Teacher Education*, 10 (1–2): 63–87.

Godwin, S. and Sutherland, R. (2004) 'Whole-Class Technology for Learning Mathematics: The Case of Functions and Graphs', *Education, Communications and Information*, 4 (1): 131–53.

Goffman, E. (1959) *The Presentation of the Self in Everyday Life*. Garden City, NY: Doubleday.

Gokhale, A. A. (1995) 'Collaborative Learning Enhances Critical Thinking', *Journal of Technology Education*, 7 (1), available online at http://scholar.lib.vt.edu/ejournals/JTE/V7n1 (accessed 28 June 2006).

Goodison, T. A. M. (2002) 'Learning with ICT at Primary Level: Pupils' Perceptions', *Journal of Computer Assisted Learning*, 18: 282–95.

Goodson, I.F. (1993) *School Subjects and Curriculum Change*, London: Falmer.

—— (1997) *Studying Curriculum: Cases and Methods*, Buckingham: Open University Press.

—— and Mangan, J. M. (1995) 'Subject Cultures and the Introduction of Classroom Computers', *British Educational Research Journal*, 21 (5): 613–28.

—— and Marsh, C. J. (1998) *Studying School Subjects: A Guide*, London: Routledge.

Goodwyn, A. (1997) *Developing English Teachers*, Buckingham: Open University Press.

—— (2000) *English in the Digital Age: Information and Communications Technology and the Teaching of English*, London: RoutledgeFalmer.

Graves, D. (1983) *Writing: Teachers and Children at Work*, Portsmouth, NH: Heinemann.

Gregoire, R., Bracewell, R. and Lafarriere, T. (1996) 'The Contribution of New Technologies to Learning and Technology in Elementary and Secondary School', available online at http://www.tact.fse.unlaval.ca/fr/html/impactnt.html (accessed 20 July 2006).

Grossman, P. (1990) *The Making of a Teacher: Teacher Knowledge and Teacher Education*, New York: Teachers College Press.

Guardian Education (2001) 'The School We'd Like', 5 June, available online at http://www.guardian.co.uk/guardianeducation/story/0,3605,501372,00.html (accessed 23 June 2006).

Halliday, M.A.K., (1975) *Learning How to Mean: Explorations in the development of language*, London: Edward Arnold.

Hartley, D. (1998) *Re-Schooling Society?*, Milton Keynes: Open University Press.

Haydn, T. (2002) 'Subject discipline dimensions of ICT and learning: history, a case study', *International Journal of Historical Learning, Teaching and Research*, 2(1): 17–36.

—— (2003) 'Introduction', in T. Haydn and C. Counsell (eds), *History, ICT and Learning in the Secondary School*, London: RoutledgeFalmer pp. 1–10.

help2learn Available online at http://www.Help2learn.co.uk (accessed 1 September 2006).

Heppell, Stephen (2007) 'A Whole New Way of Thinking', *Education Guardian*, 9 January, available online at http://education.guardian.co.uk/elearning/story/0,,1985421,00.html (accessed on 8 November 2007).

Hicks, P. and Bishop, J. (2005) 'Schools Without Walls', in S. Wheeler (ed.), *Transforming Primary ICT*, Exeter: Learning Matters, pp. 175–86.

Higgins, S. (2003) *Does ICT Improve Learning and Teaching in Schools?*, Nottingham: British Educational Research Association.

Howe, C., Tolmie, A. and Mckenzie, M. (1996) 'Computer Support for the Collaborative Learning of Physics Concepts', in C. O'Malley (ed.), *Computer Simulated Collaborative Learning*, Berlin: Springer Verlag, pp. 51–68.

Hoyle, E. and John, P. D. (1995) *Professional Knowledge and Professional Practice*, London: Cassell.

Hoyles, C., Healy, L. and Pozzi, S. (1994) 'Group Work with Computers: An Overview of Findings', *Journal of Computer Assisted Learning*, 109 (4): 202–13.

Hyland, K. (2003) *Second Language Writing*, Cambridge: Cambridge University Press.

Interactive Education Project (2005) Reference

Jay, T. (1981) 'Computerphobia: What to Do About It', *Educational Technology*, 21: 47–8.

Jilani, H. (2003) 'Human Rights Defenders and Democratization', paper presented to the fifth International Conference of New or Restored Democracies, Ulaanbaatar, Mongolia, 10–12 September, available online at http://www.ohchr.org/english/issues/defenders/democracy.htm (accessed 30 June 2006).

John, P. D. (2005) 'The Sacred and the Profane: Subject Sub-Culture, Pedagogical Practice and Teachers' Perceptions of the Classroom Uses of ICT', *Educational Review*, 57 (4): 471–91.

—— and La Velle, L. B. (2004) 'Devices and Desires: Subject Subcultures, Pedagogical Identity and the Challenge of Information and Communications Technology', *Technology, Pedagogy and Education*, 13 (3): 307–26.

Johnson, D. W., and Johnson, R. T. (1989) *Cooperation and Competition: Theory and Research*, Edina, Minn.: Interaction Book Company.

Johnson, M. (2004) *Personalised Learning: An Emperor's Outfit?*, London: Institute for Public Policy Research.

John-Steiner, V. and Mahn, H. (1996) 'Socio-Cultural Approaches to Learning and Development', *Educational Psychologist*, 31: 191–206.

Jonassen, D. H., Peck, K. L. and Wilson, B. G. (1999) *Learning with Technology: A Constructivist Perspective*, Columbus, OH: Merrill Prentice Hall.

Kahney, H. (1993) *Problem Solving: Current Issues*, 2nd edn, Buckingham: Open University Press.

Kelly, K. (2003) 'New Independence for Special Needs Students', in T. Gordon (ed.) *The Digital Classroom*, Cambridge, Mass.: The Harvard Education Letter, pp. 36–48.

Kelly, Ruth (2005) Foreword to 'Harnessing Technology: Transforming Learning and Children's Services', available online at http://www.dfes.gov.uk/publications/e-strategy/docs/e-strategy.pdf

Kennewell, S. (2001) 'Interactive Whiteboards: Yet Another Solution in Search of a Problem to Solve', *Information Technology in Teacher Education*, 39: 3–6.

Kerr, A. (1991) 'Lever and Fulcrum: Educational Technologies in Teachers Thought and Practice', *Teachers College Record*, 93 (1): 114–36.

Khaleej Times (2004) 'Women Call Misuse of Camera Phones Invasion of Privacy', available online at http://www.khaleejtimes.com/displayarticle.asp?section=theuaeandxfile=data/theuae/2004/july/theuae_july517.xml (accessed 19 June 2006).

Knight, B. A. and Knight, C. (1995) 'Cognitive Theory and the Use of Computers in the Primary Classroom', *British Journal of Educational Technology*, 26: 141–8.

Kress, G. (2000) 'Multimodality', in B. Cope and M. Kalantzis (eds) *Multiliteracies: Literacy Learning and the Design of Social Futures*, London: Routledge, pp. 182–202.

Kumar, V. S. (1996) 'Theories of Learning and Cognition in Collaboration', available online at http://www.cs.usask.ca/grads/vsk719/academic/890/project2/node7.html (accessed 28 June 2006).

La Velle, L., Mcfarlane, A., John, P. D. and Brawn, R. (2004) 'According to the Promises: The Sub-Culture of School Science, Teachers' Pedagogic Identity and the Challenge of ICT', *Education, Communication and Information*, 4 (1): 109–31.

Lacey, C. (1977) *The Socialisation of Teachers*, London: Methuen.

Lankshear, C. and Knobel, M. (2003) *New Literacies: Changing Knowledge and Classroom Learning*, Buckingham: Open University Press.

Latham, P. (2002) 'Teaching and Learning Primary Mathematics: The Impact of Interactive Whiteboards', available online at http://www.beam.co.uk/pdfs/RES03.pdf (accessed 21 November 2007).

Latour, B. (1999) *Pandora's Hope. Essays on the Reality of Science Studies*, Cambridge, MA and London: Harvard University Press.

Lave, J. and Wenger, E. (1991) *Situated Learning: Legitimate Peripheral Participation*, Cambridge: Cambridge University Press.

Learning and Teaching Scotland (2006) 'ICT and Inclusion', available online at http://www.ltscotland.org.uk/inclusiveeducation/ictandinclusion/index.asp (accessed 20 July 2006).

Lee, M. and Boyle, M. (2003) 'The Educational Effects and Implications of the Interactive Whiteboard Strategy of Richardson Primary School', Richardson Primary School: ACT, Australia, available online at http://www.Richardsonps.Act.Edu.Au/Richardsonreview_Grey.pdf (accessed 12 October 2005).

Levinson, P. (2003) *Real Space*, London: Routledge.

Levy, P. (2002) *Interactive Whiteboards in Learning and Teaching in Two Sheffield Schools: A Development Study*, Sheffield: Department of Information Studies, University of Sheffield.

Light, P., Littlejohn, K., Messer, D. and Johnson, R. (1996) 'Social Communicative Processes and Computer Based Problem Solving', *European Journal of Psychology of Education*, 7 (4): 1–14.

Loveless, A. and Ellis, V. (eds) (2001) *ICT, Pedagogy and the Curriculum*, London and New York: RoutledgeFalmer.

Mcfarlane, A. (1997) 'The Effectiveness of ILS', in J. Underwood and J. Brown (eds), *Integrated Learning Systems: Potential into Practice*, Oxford: Heinemann, pp. 15–29.

Mckinsey and Company (1997) *The Future of Information Technology in UK Schools*, London: McKinsey and Company.

Mcluhan, M. (1964) *Understanding Media*, New York: McGraw-Hill.

Mander, J. (1991) *In the Absence of the Sacred*, New York: Sierra Club Books.

Mandinach, E. B. and Cline, H. F. (1994) *Classroom Dynamics: Implementing a Technology Based Learning Environment*, Hillside, NJ: Lawrence Erlbaum Associates.

Maor, D. and Taylor, P. C. (1995) 'Teacher Epistemology and Scientific Inquiry in Computerised Classroom Environments', *Journal of Research in Science Teaching*, 32: 839–54.

Matthewman, S. and Triggs, P. (2004) 'Obsessive Compulsive Font Disorder: The Challenge of Supporting Children's Writing with the Computer', *Computers and Education*, 43: 125–35.

Miliband, David (2004a) Minister of State for School Standards at the North of England Education Conference in Belfast, January.

—— (2004b) 'Choice and Voice in Personalised Learning', speech by David Miliband MP at the DfES Innovation Unit/Demos/OECD Conference, London, 18 May.

Miller, D. and Glover, D. (2002) 'Running with technology: The impact of the large-scale introduction of interactive whiteboards in one secondary school', *Journal of Information Technology for Teacher Education*, 10(3), 257–76.

——, —— and Averis, D. (2004) 'Motivation: The Contribution of Interactive Whiteboards to Teaching and Learning in Mathematics', available online at http://cerme4.crm.es/Papers%20definitius/9/Miller-Glover-Averis.pdf (accessed 8 November 2007).

Molyneaux, S. (2003) 'Keynote Speech to the Plymouth E-Learning Conference', University of Plymouth, November.

Moore, A. (2003) *The Good Teacher: Dominant Discourses in Teaching and Teacher Education*, London: Routledge Falmer.

Morris, Estelle (2001) 'Information on Education Expenditure According to Parliamentary . . . and of the Same Value as Other Individual Learning Accounts', House of Commons, Hansard Written Answered, 29 January, available online at http://www.publications.parliament.uk/pa/cm200001/cmhansrd/vo010129/text/10129w08.htm (accessed 8 November 2007).

Morrison, D. (2003) 'From Chalkface to Interface: The impact of the Interactive Whiteboards in the history of the classroom', available online at http://www.ltscotland.org.uk/connected/articles/8/specialfeature/chalkfacetointerface.asp (accessed 21 November 2007).

Moseley, L. (1999) *Ways Forward with ICT: Effective Pedagogy Using Information and Communications Technology for Literacy and Numeracy in Primary Schools*, Newcastle: University of Newcastle.

Moyles, J., Hargreaves, L., Merry, R., Paterson, F. and Estarte-Sarries, V. (2003) *Interactive Teaching in the Primary School: Digging Deeper into Meanings*, Oxford: Oxford University Press.

Muirhead, G., Hicks, P. and Bishop, J. (2005) 'Schools of the Future', in S. Wheeler (ed.), *Transforming Primary ICT*, Exeter: Learning Matters, pp. 161–86.

Mumtaz, S. (2000) 'Factors Affecting Teachers' Use of Information and Communications Technology: A Review of the Literature', *Journal of Information Technology for Teacher Education*, 9 (3): 319–41.

Nash, R. (1973) *Classrooms Observed: The Teacher's Perception and the Pupil's Performance*, London: Routledge and Kegan Paul.

National Audit Office, available online at http://www.nao.org.uk (accessed 5 June, 2007).

National Statistics Office (2005) Available online at http://www.statistics.gov.uk (accessed 18 July 2006).

Norman, D. A. (1990) *The Design of Everyday Things*, New York: Doubleday.

—— (1993) *Things That Make Us Smart: Defending Human Attributes in the Age of the Machine*, New York: Basic Books.

—— (1999) *The Invisible Computer: Why Good Products Can Fail, the Personal Computer is so Complex and Information Appliances are the Solution*, Cambridge, Mass.: MIT Press.

—— (2004) *Emotional Design: Why We Love or Hate Everyday Things*, Basic Books: New York.

Northern Grid for Learning (2006) Available online at http://www.portal.northerngrid.org.

Noss, R. and Hoyles, C. (1996a) 'The Visibility of Meanings: Modelling the Mathematics of Banking', *International Journal of Computers for Mathematical Learning*, 1 (1): 3–31.

—— and —— (1996b) *Windows on Mathematical Meanings: Learning Cultures and Computers*, Boston, Mass.: Kluwer Academic Press.

—— and Pachler, N. (1999) 'The Challenge of New Technologies: Doing Old Things in a New Way or Doing New Things?', in P. Mortimore (ed.), *Understanding Pedagogy and Its Impact on Learning*, London: Sage, 195–211.

Ober, R. L., Bentley, E. L. and Miller, E. (1971) *Systematic Observation of Teaching*, Englewood Cliffs, NJ: Prentice Hall.

Ofsted (2001) 'ICT in schools: The impact of government initiatives. An interim report', London: Ofsted.

—— (2004) 'ICT in schools: The impact of government initiatives five years on', available online at http://www.ofsted.gov.uk/portal/site/Internet/menuitem.eace3f09a603f6d9c3172a8a08c08a0c/?vgnextoid=f7b51e7a681eb010VgnVCM2000003607640aRCRD (accessed 21 November 2007).

Ong, W. (1982) *Orality and Literacy*, London: Routledge.

Oseas, A. and Wood, J. M. (2003) 'Multiple Literacies: New Skills for a New Millennium', in D. T. Gordon (ed.), *Better Teaching and Learning in the Digital Classroom*, Cambridge, Mass.: Harvard Education Press, pp. 11–16.

Panitz, T. (1996) 'A Definition of Collaborative vs. Cooperative Learning', available online at http://www.city.londonmet.ac.uk/deliberations/collab.learning/panitz2.html (accessed 28 June 2006).

Papert, Seymour (2006) 'Foreword', in M. Resnick, *Turtles, Termites and Traffic Jams: Explorations in a Massively Parallel Microworlds*, Cambridge, Mass.: MIT Press.

Parker, M. and Townsend, M. (2005) 'It's What I Do Already: Becoming a Higher Level Teaching Assistant', paper presented at the British Educational Research Association Conference, University of Glamorgan, 15–17 September.

Pavely, S. (1999) 'Advocacy and Self-Advocacy', in M. Blamires (ed.), *Enabling Technology for Inclusion*, London: Paul Chapman Publishing, pp. 37–51.

Pea, R. (1985) 'Beyond Amplification: Using the Computer to Reorganise Mental Functioning', *Educational Psychologist*, 20: 167–82.

Piaget, J. (1954) *The Construction of Reality in the Child*, New York: Basic Books.

Pittard, V. (2004) 'Evidence for e-learning policy', *Technology, Pedagogy and Education*, 13(2), pp. 181–94.

Plowman, L., Stephen, C., Downey, S. and Sime, D. (2006) 'Supporting Learning with ICT in Pre-School Settings. Teaching and Learning Research Programme Research Briefing Number 15. ESRC', available online at http://www.tlrp.org (accessed 25 June 2006).

Postman, N. (1992) *Technopoly*, New York: Knopf.

Prensky, M. (2001) 'Digital Natives, Digital Immigrants' *On the Horizon*, 9 (5): 1–6, available online at http://www.marcprensky.com/writing/Prensky%20-%20Digital%20Natives,%20Digital%20Immigrants%20-%20Part1.pdf (accessed 19 July 2006).

Primary National Strategy (2006), available online at http://www.standards.dfes.gov.uk (accessed 8 November 2007).

Preston, C., Cox, M. J. and Cox, K. M. (2000) 'Teachers as Innovators: An Evaluation of the Motivation of Teachers to Use Information and Communications Technologies', in M. Cox, C. Abbott, M. Webb, B. Blakeley, T. Beauchamp and V. Rhodes (eds) (2003), *ICT and Attainment: A Review of the Research Literature*, Norwich: DfES.

PricewaterhouseCoopers (2001) 'The Teacher Workload Study', available online at http://www.teachernet.gov.uk/docbank/index.cfm?id=3165 (accessed 21 November 2007).

PricewaterhouseCoopers (2002) 'Good practice in cutting bureaucracy: Reducing bureaucratic burdens', London: DfES.

QCA (2005) 'Guide to P-Scales National Data Collection', available online at http://www.qca.org.uk/qca_8545.aspx (accessed 8 November 2007).

Reynolds, D. (1998) 'Schooling For Literacy: A Review of Research on Teacher Effectiveness and School Effectiveness and Its Implications for Contemporary Educational Policies', *Educational Review*, 50 (2): 147–62.

—— and Farrell, S. (1996) *Worlds Apart? A Review of International Surveys of Educational Achievement in England*, London: HMSO.

Rogers, E. M. (1983) *Diffusion of Innovation*, 3rd edn, New York: Macmillan.

Rogoff, B. (1984) 'Introduction: Thinking and Learning in a Social Context', in B. Rogoff and J. Lave (eds), *Everyday Cognition: Developing Learning in a Social Context*, Cambridge: Cambridge University Press, pp. 1–8.

—— (1995) 'Observing Socio-Cultural Activity on Three Planes: Participatory Appropriation, Guided Participation and Apprenticeship', in J. Wertsch, P. Del Rio and A. Alvarez (eds), *Sociocultural Studies of Mind*, Cambridge: Cambridge University Press, pp. 139–64.

Rose, R. (2000) 'Developing a Partnership in Learning', in C. Tilstone, L. Florian and R. Rose (eds), *Promoting Inclusive Practice*, London: RoutledgeFalmer, pp. 95–112.

Ruthven, K., Hennessy, S. and Brindley, S. (2004) 'Teachers' Representations of the Successful Use of Computer-Based Tools and Resources in Secondary English, Mathematics and Science', *Teaching and Teacher Education*, 20 (3): 259–75.

St Helens Council, Curriculum and ICT Resources, available online at http://www.sthelens.org.uk/teachers/curriculum/ict/resour/selfases/selasses1.htm (accessed 1 September 2006).

Sandholz, J. H., Ringstaff, C. and Dwyer, D. C. (1996) *Teaching with Technology: Creating Pupil Centred Classrooms*, New York: Teachers College Press.

Schön, D. (1987) *Educating the Reflective Practitioner*, San Francisco, Calif.: Jossey-Bass.

Scott, J. (2004) 'The Great Failure of Wikipedia', available online at http://ascii.textfiles.com/archives/000060.html (accessed 21 August 2006).

Scrimshaw, P. (1997) *Using Information Technology Effectively in Teaching and Learning: Studies in Pre-Service and In-Service Teacher Education*, London: Routledge.

Sefton-Green, J. (2005) 'A Brave New Digital World is Outside the School Gates', *Connected* 13, available online at http://www.ltscotland.org.uk/ictineducation/Connected (accessed 25 June 2006).

Selinger, M. (1994) 'Understanding', in M. Selinger (ed.) *Teaching Mathematics*, London: Routledge, pp. 185–94.

—— (2002) 'Learning Computer Technology Skills in the Subject Context of Learning', *Journal of Information Technology for Teacher Education*, 10 (1–2): 143–57.

Selwyn, N. (1999) 'Differences in Educational Computer Use: The Influence of Subject Cultures', *The Curriculum Journal*, 12 (1): 11–29.

——, Dawes, L. and Mercer, N. (2001) 'Promoting Mr "Chips": The Construction of the Teacher–Computer Relationship in Educational Advertising', *Teaching and Teacher Education*, 17 (4): 3–14.

Simonson, M. and Wheeler, S. (2003) 'Final Report of the Evaluation Team of the South Dakota Alliance for Distance Education', Department of Education and Cultural Affairs, State of South Dakota, available online at http://www2.plymouth.ac.uk/distancelearning/finalreport.pdf (accessed 21 June 2006).

Smith, H. (2001) *Smartboard Evaluation: Final Report*. Kent: NGfL.

——, Higgins, S., Wall, K. and Miller, J. (2005) 'Interactive Whiteboards: Boon or Bandwagon? A Critical Review of the Literature', *Journal of Computer Assisted Learning*, 21: 91–101.

Somekh, B. (1992) 'Calling Whose Bluff? Some Responses of Initial Teacher Educators to Information Technology', *Cambridge Journal of Education*, 22 (2): 157–62.

Special Educational Needs and Disability Act, Chapter 10 (2001) Available online at http://www.opsi.gov.uk/acts/acts2001/20010010.htm (accessed 5 June 2006).

Strauss, A. and Corbin, J. M. (1990) *Basics of Qualitative Research*, Newbury Park, Calif.: Sage Publications.

Stubbs, M. (1976) *Language, Schools and Classrooms*, London: Methuen.

Sutherland, R., Armstrong, V. Barnes, S., Brawn, R., Gall, M., Matthewman, S., Olivero, F., Taylor, A., Triggs, P., Wishart, J. and John, P. (2004) 'Transforming Teaching and Learning: Embedding ICT into Every-Day Classroom Practices', *Journal of Computer Assisted Learning Special Issue*, 20 (6): 413–25.

——, John, P. D. and Robertson, S. (eds) (forthcoming) *Improving ICT and Learning*, London: Gateway Books.

Tapscott, D. (1998) *Growing Up Digital: The Rise of the Net Generation*, New York: McGraw-Hill.

Taylor, E. W. (1998) *The Theory and Practice of Transformative Learning: A Critical Review of Information*, Series Number 374, Columbus, OH: Ohio State University.

Teachernet 'Extended Schools', available online at http://www.teachernet.gov.uk/wholeschool/extendedschools (accessed 12 July 2006).

—— 'The Classroom of the Future', available online at http://www.teachernet.gov.uk/management/resourcesfinanceandbuilding/schoolbuildings/sbschoolsforthefuture/futureclassrooms (accessed 12 July 2006).

—— (2001) 'The SEN Code of Practice', available online at http://www.teachernet.gov.uk/docbank/index.cfm?id=3724 (accessed 12 July 2006).

—— (2006) 'The SEN Toolkit', available online at http://www.teachernet.gov.uk/wholeschool/sen/teacherlearningassistant/toolkit (accessed 12 July 2006).

Teachers TV (2006) 'Get Organised', available online at http://www.teachers.tv/subjectblock programme.do?transmissionblockid=278291andzoneid=1andtransmissionprogrammeid=277774 1 (accessed 11 July 2006).

Thomas Danby College (2004) 'E-Learning and Technology Project', available online at http://www.learningtechnologies.ac.uk/ask/users (accessed 20 June 2006).

Thompson, B. (2004) 'A Question of Trust Online', BBC News, April 23, available online at http://news.bbc.co.uk/2/hi/technology/3653425.stm (accessed 20 August 2006).

Tinzmann, M. B., Jones, B. F., Fennimore, T. F., Bakker, J., Fine, C. and Pierce, J. (1990) 'What is the Collaborative Classroom? North Central Regional Educational Laboratory', available online at http://www.ncrel.org/sdrs/areas/rpl_esys/collab.htm (accessed 28 June 2006).

Tools for Schools (2004) Available online at http://www.e-skills.com/cgi-bin/go.pl/news/news.html?uid=325 (accessed 12 July 2006).

Topping, K. and Maloney, S. (eds) (2005) *The RoutledgeFalmer Reader in Inclusive Education*, Abingdon: RoutledgeFalmer.

Totten, S., Sills, T., Digby, A. and Russ, P. (1991) *Cooperative Learning: A Guide to Research*, New York: Garland.

Townsend, M. (2005) 'Meeting Individual Differences: Using ICT to Support Communication Skills for Children with Learning Difficulties', in S. Wheeler (ed.), *Transforming Primary ICT*, Exeter: Learning Matters, pp. 94–113.

—— and Parker, M. (2006) 'Changing Times, Changing Roles: Evaluating the Impact of Higher Level Teaching Assistants on Learning and Teaching in the Classroom', paper presented at the British Educational Research Association Conference, Warwick University, 6–9 September.

Triggs, P. and John, P. D. (2004) 'From Transaction to Transformation: Information and Communication Technology, Professional Development and the Formation of Communities of Practice', *Journal of Computer Assisted Learning*, 20 (6): 426–39.

—— and Matthewman, S. (2004) 'Obsessive compulsive font disorder: the challenge of supporting pupils writing with the computer', *Computers and Education*, 43(1–2), 125–35.

UNESCO (2004) 'The Salamanca Statement and Framework for Action on Special Needs Education', paper adopted by World Conference on Special Needs Education: Access and Quality. Salamanca, Spain 7–10 June, 2004, available online at http://www.unesco.org/education/pdf/salama_e.pdf (accessed 12 June 2006).

Vaughan, S. (1997) 'Number Education for Very Young Children: Can IT Change the Nature of Early Years Mathematics Education?', in N. Davis and B. Somekh (eds), *Using IT Effectively in Teaching and Learning*, London: Routledge, pp. 40–49.

Venezky, R. L. (2004) 'Technology in the Classroom: Steps Toward a New Vision', *Education, Communication and Information*, 4 (1): 3–21.

Visual Impairment Scotland Research 'Using New Developments in Chatroom Technology as a Tool for Inclusion', available online at http://www.ssc.education.ed.ac.uk/research/viandmulti/chat.html (accessed 20 June 2006).

Vygotsky, L. S. (1978) *Mind in Society: The Development of Higher Psychological Processes*, Cambridge, Mass.: Harvard University Press.

Waite, S., Wheeler, S. and Bromfield, C. (2007) 'Our Flexible Friend: The Implications of Individual Differences for Information Technology', *Computers and Education*, 48 (1): 80–99.

Walker, D. (2002) 'White Enlightening', *Times Educational Supplement*, 13 September.

Walsh, B. (1998) 'Why Gerry Likes History Now: The Power of the Word Processor', *Teaching History*, 93: 6–15.

Watson, D. M. (2001) 'Pedagogy Before Technology: Rethinking the Relationship Between ICT and Teaching', *Education and Information Technologies*, 6 (4): 251–66.

Watson, G. (2002) 'Models of Information Technology Teacher Professional Development that Engage Teachers' Hearts and Minds', *Journal of Information Technology for Teacher Education*, 10 (1–2): 179–91.

Webb, N. (1985) 'Student Interaction and Learning in Small Groups: A Research Summary', cited in A. A. Gokhale (1995) 'Collaborative Learning Enhances Critical Thinking', *Journal of Technology Education*, 7 (1), available online at http://scholar.lib.vt.edu/ejournals/jte/v7n1 (accessed 28 June 2006).

Wenger, E. (1990) 'Toward a Theory of Cultural Transparency: Elements of a Social Discourse of the Visible and the Invisible', unpublished Ph.D. dissertation, University of California at Irvine, and IRL-Monograph 91–0007.

Wertsch, J. (1998) *Mind as Action*, New York: Oxford University Press.

Westheimer, J. and Kahn, J. (1993) 'Building a School Community: An Experienced Based Model', *Phi Delta Kappan*, 75: 324–8.

Wheeler, S. (2000) 'User Reactions to Videoconferencing: Which Students Cope Best?' *Educational Media International*, 37 (1): 31–8.

—— (2001) 'Information and Communication Technologies and the Changing Role of the Teacher', *Journal of Educational Media*, 26 (1): 7–18.

—— (ed.) (2005) *Transforming Primary ICT*, Exeter: Learning Matters.

—— and Boulos, M. N. K. (2006) 'Do You Have a Wiki Side? Evaluation of the Wiki As an Educational Tool', paper presented at the Association for Learning Technologies Conference (ALT-C), Heriot Watt University, Edinburgh, 4–6 September.

—— and Winter, A. (2005) 'ICT: Winning Hearts and Minds', in S. Wheeler (ed.), *Transforming Primary ICT*, Exeter: Learning Matters.

——, Waite, S. and Bromfield (2002) 'Promoting Creative Thinking through the Use of ICT', *Journal of Computer Assisted Learning*, 180 (3): 367–78.

Whelan, R. (2000) 'How schools can get the most from their information resources', European Schoolnet.

Williams, P. (2005) 'Lessons from the future: ICT scenarios and the education of teachers', *Journal of Education for Teaching: International Research and Pedagogy*, 31 (4), pp. 319–39.

Wilson, V., Schlapp, U. and Davidson, J. (2003) 'An Extra Pair of Hands? Managing Classroom Assistants in Scottish Primary Schools', *Education Management and Administration*, 31 (2): 189–205.

Wineburg, S. and Grossman, P. (1998). 'Creating a Community of Learners Among High School Teachers', *Phi Delta Kappan* (January): 350–3.

Wokingham District Council, ICT Record, available online at http://www.supporting-Ict.co.uk (accessed 20 March 2006).

Wood, C. (2001) 'Interactive Whiteboards: A Luxury Too Far?', *Teaching ICT* 1(2), 52–62.

Wood, T. A. (1999) 'Psychological Access and the Internet', in G. Cummings (ed.), *Advanced Research in Computers in Education*, Ohmsha: Los Press, pp. 973–980.

Woolgar, S. (1988) *Science, the Very Idea*, New York: Tavistock Publishing.

Index

Page numbers in *italic* denote tables or figures.

'age-appropriateness' 68–9
ALIS 29
'analogues' 125
Andrews, R. 81
assessment 29, 60, 71–9; barriers to effective 76–7, 79; and data trackers 33; models of 73–5; criterion-referenced 74; diagnostic 73; formative 73–4; ipsative 75; norm-referenced 74; peer 75; self- 74–5, 77–8; summative 74; triadic 75; nature of 71–3; reasons for necessity of 72–3; and record-keeping 77–9; and reliability issue 76; use of ICT as tool for 77–9; and validity issue 76
attention deficit 91
Attewell, Jill 115
autistic spectrum disorder (ASD) 58–9
automaticity: and ICT 67–70

Baby Boomers 126, *126*
Baker, Kenneth 7
Ball, D.L. 118
BARE programme 60
Barnes, D.: *From Communication to Curriculum* 46
Barnett, M. 81
Baudrillard, J. 2
Beard, R. 46
Bebo 27
Becta 21–2, 23, 32, 48–9
Birch, J. 50
Blair, Tony 6, 7, 11–12, 26
blended learning 35
blogs 128
Bluetooth application 77
Bristol Dyslexia Centre website 61

British Educational Computing and Technology Agency 58
Brosnan, M. 109
Brown, Stephen 47
Bruner, Jerome 40, 118

CAL *see* computer-assisted learning
Castells, M. 7
CATs 29
Centre for Studies in Inclusive Education (CSIE) 56
Chandler, P. 121
Chapelle, C.A. 36
chatrooms 68
choice: and SEN 65–6
Clarke, Charles 26
classroom: as a community 120
Classroom of the Future project 69
classroom practices 55
cognition, modes of 4
cognitive development, zones of 39–40
cognitive overload 121
collaboration: as a catalyst for creative thinking 40–1; enhancement of by ICT 80, 117; as a scaffold for learning 40
collaborative learning 38–44, 115, 121; and construction of knowledge 39; definitions 39; and digital cameras 42–3; mind tools and social networks 41; wiki spaces 41–2; and zones of cognitive development 39–40
Community of Learning project 118–19
compatibility issues: and use of ICT 97–8
competence: and confidence 122; lack of as barrier to ICT 22
computer room 87, 93
computer-aided assessment (CAA) 74
computer-assisted learning (CAL) 15–16, 41

computers 41, 62; accessing of by special needs children 62–3; at home 106–7; automaticity and provisionality 67–70; and digitisation 3; flexibility of 62; personal 99, *100*; software compatability 97; usability issue 98; use of as mind tools 41
concurrent validity 76
confidence: and competence 122; lack of as barrier to ICT 22
congruence: and learning 88–90
Connecting the Learning Society 8, 9, 11–12
construct validity 76
continuing professional development (CPD) 117–23
Counsell, C. 88
Cox, M.J. *et al.* 23
creative thinking 38; collaboration as a catalyst for 40–1
criterion-referenced assessment 74
cultural transparency 82, 90, 125
curriculum 80–92, 121; congruence and learning 88–90; individual 29–30; new technologies and 80–92; non-technological issues hindering extended use of ICT in subject areas 90; online 33; physical barriers in using ICT 87; research study into ICT and 82–7; subject areas and new technology 81–2; subject pedagogy and ICT 86–7, 91–2; *see also* National Curriculum

Dale, R. *et al.* 7, 8
data projectors 51, 52, 98
data trackers 27, 33
Davis, B. and Sumara, D. 119
DfES (Department for Education and Skills) 9, 10, 57, 65; 'Personalised learning' initiative 63; White Paper (2005) 65
diagnostic assessment 73
diagnostic software 77
diffusion of innovation 99–100, *100*
digital cameras 16, 42–3, 98, *100*
digital classroom: construction of 93–104
digital divide 106–7
digital immigrants 125, 126
digital literacy 127
digital natives 67, 125, 126
digital television 99–100, *100*
Directgov web site 58
Down's Syndrome 66
Down's Syndrome Information Network 58

'drill and practice' 15
Dwyer, D.C. *et al.* 119–20, 123
dyslexia 61

e-learning 9, 10, 23
e-learning credits *24*
e-mail 34, 127; and home-school links 110; and school magazines 37
'e-mail an author' 37
'e-mail a Viking' 37
e-portfolios 27, 33, 34
e-Strategy document 9–10, 12–13
early adopters 99, *100*, 115
economic imperatives: and information technology 7, 8, 9
electromagnetic whiteboards 47
electronic 'distance' 69
electronic writing frame 36
empirical validity 76
'Encarta syndrome' 16
English/English teachers: and ICT 81, 84, 85, 89, 121
enthusiasts 2, 17
Eraut, M. 46, 92
ESRC InterActive Education Project 30–1
European Union: Education Council 7
evaluation *see* assessment
Every Child Matters agenda 28
experiential mode 4, 5
'extended schools' 33 *see also* home-school links

face validity 76
Facebook 27
Fairbrother, B. and Harrison, C. 74
feedback 37; and assessment 72
fit for purpose 98, 102
Fitzpatrick, G. 28
flexible time 23
flexibility: of hardware and software 23
Flickr 27
focus groups 58
'folk pedagogy' 118
'folksonomies' 8
foreign languages *see* modern foreign languages
Forman, E.A. and Cazden, C.B. 40
formative approach 29–30
formative assessment 73–4
Fox, B. 74
functionalism 17

Gamble, N. and Easingwood, N. 37
Gates, Bill 114
Generation Xers 126, *126*
Germany: personalised learning 29
Giangreco, M.F. 59
Giddens, A. 28
Gobbo, C. and Girardi, G. 119
Goffman, E. 28
Goodison, T.A.M. 50
Goodson, I.F. 80; and Mangan, J.M. 81
Goodwyn, A. 85
graphics pads, wireless 48
Gregoire, R. *et al.* 118
Grossman, P. 119
group learning 37
Guardian 69

HABET (Historical Association's advisory
    body on educational technology) 85
'handheld learning' 115
hardware 8–9, *24*; flexibility of 23
'Harnessing Technology' 12–13, 21
Hartley, D. 123
headteachers: and Government's ICT strategy
    8
help2learn 79
Heppell, Stephen 30
Hicks, P. and Bishop, J. 77
higher level teaching assistants (HLTAs)
    60–1
history: and ICT 85, 121
Home School Agreement 109
home use: and ICT 84
home-school links 105–6, 109–11; creating
    web presence 110–11; and e-mail 110; and
    mobile phones 115–16
homework diaries 33
Hoyles, C. *et al.* 121
humanities 81
Huxley, Aldous: *Brave New World* 4–5
Hyland, K. 36
hyperlinks 65

ICT (information and communication
    technology): enhancement of in-school
    learning 32–3; enhancement of out-of-
    school learning 33–4; issues influencing
    success or failure of adoption of 97–9;
    positive factors needed for successful
    implementation of *24*; practical tips 103;
    reasons for failure in schools 95;
    requirements for successful change

management 102–3; teaching about and
    teaching through 50, 120–1
ICT coordinator 103–4, 128
ICT suites 93–4
impact stage 99
in-school technology 32–3
inclusion 55–70; automaticity and
    provisionality 67–70; in context 56;
    features of successful 59; key elements in
    maintaining effective pathway to 60;
    macro-political operational level 56–7;
    micro-operational level 56, 62–6;
    micro-political operational level 56,
    59–60; *see also* SEN
independent learning 37
individual curriculum: and personalised
    learning 29–30
Industrial Revolution 1
information and communication technology
    see ICT
innovation diffusion 99–100
interaction trajectories: and personalised
    learning 30–1
InterActive Education Project 51, 82,
    90
'Interactive logbook' 34
interactive teaching 46–7
interactive technologies 45–54; and literacy
    strategies 51–4; and mathematics teaching
    51; *see also* IWBs
interactive whiteboard *see* IWBs
interface 62
Internet 3, 16, 27, 55, 65, 106, 128; benefits
    of 16; gaining information on SEN by
    parents 58–9; and government 57–8; and
    home-school links 110–11; interactive
    nature of 58; as the medium of media 106;
    parental concerns over use of 107; and
    social interaction 27–8
iPods 35
ipsative assessment 75
IWB tablets 48
IWBs (interactive whiteboards) 5, 16, 30,
    45–51, 95; accessibility 48; advantages in
    terms of 'facing the class' 50; basics of
    technology 47; benefits 45, 48–9, 49–50;
    flexibility 48, 49; functionality 47–8, 49;
    and literacy 49, 52–3; research evidence
    48–50

John, P.D. 21; and La Velle, L.B. 81
Johnson, M. 30

Joint Information Systems Committee (JISC) 34

Jonassen, David 41

joysticks 62

Kelly, Ruth 12–13, 21

keyboards 48, 62–3; and SEN 62–3

knowledge 119; construction of 39

knowledge economy 6

laggards 99, *101*

laptops 87

laser-scanner whiteboards 47

Lave, J. 82; and Wenger, E. 120

learners 23

learning: full involvement of pupils in 62–3; and new technology 3–5

learning difficulties *see* inclusion; SEN

learning styles 52, 63

Learning and Teaching Scotland 58

'lease-hire' schemes 99

liberalism 17

lifelong learning 7, 21, 117

literacy: digital 127; and ICT 51–4; and IWBs 49, 52–3; national strateg 30, 46, 51

literacy hour 37

logbook, interactive 34

London School of Economics 105, 106

Loveless, A. and Ellis, V. 81

m-learning 115

McKinsey Report 7

McLuhan, Marshall: *Understanding Media* 2–3, 4

macro-political operational level: and inclusion 56–7

Maor, D. and Taylor, P.C. 119

mastery stage 99

mathematics: case study 36; and ICT 51, 81, 91, 121

Matthewman, S. *et al.* 49

media literacy: and ICT 53–4

Media Stage 54

Miliband, David 25–6

mind tools: and computers 41

mind-mapping software 54, 66

mobile phones 98, 100, *100*, 113–14, 115, 128; appeal of 114; disadvantages of 114; in education 115; and home-school link 115–16; ownership 112, *112*, 113–14; statistics 113

mobile technologies 111–15, 127–8; in education 115; and home-school link 115; ownership statistics 111; *see also* mobile phones

mobile wireless devices 115

modern foreign languages: case study 36; and ICT 89, 91; and IWBs 49

monitoring of progress: and assessment 72

Morris, Estelle 25

Morrison, D. 49

Moseley, L. *et al.* 54

Movie Maker 62

Moyles, J. *et al.* 46

music: and ICT 81, 85, 91

mutuality: and personalised learning 31

MySpace 27, 41

National Centre for Educational Statistics 29

National Curriculum 17, 29, 80, 81

National Grid for Learning (NGfL) 7–9, 11–12, 16

national literacy strategy 30, 46, 51

national numeracy strategy 30

Negroponte, Nick 114

New Labour 7, 25

'New Luddites' 2

New Opportunities Funding (NOF) training 9, 16

norm-referenced assessment 74

Norman, Donald 3, 4, 5, 96, 109, 125

North of England Education Conference (2004) 26

Northcote, Sydney 37

Northern Grid for Learning 64

Noss, R. and Pachler, N. 8

NotSchool initiative 34

'obsessive compulsive font disorder' 90

OfSTED (Office for Standards in Education) 45, 52

O'Leary and Parker 32–3

Omnigraph 51

online assessment tool 77

online curriculum 33

'Open for Learning, Open for Business' document 8

orality: and teachers 126–7

Orwell, George: *1984* 4–5

Oseas, A. and Wood, J.M. 127

out-of-school technology 33-4 *see also* home-school links

overlay keyboards 62

P-Scales 59, 60
Papert, Seymour 3, 5
PDAs 115
pedagogical style: importance of 121
peer assessment 75
personal computers 99, *100*
personal home pages 74
personalised learning 25–37; and blended
    learning 35; dimensions of 28–30, *28*;
    emphasis on learner and learner-driven
    outcomes 27; and individual curriculum
    29–30; and interaction between learner
    and technology 27; and interaction
    trajectories 30–1; and mutuality 31; policy
    principles 26–7; provenance of 25–6; and
    semantics 26–8; ways that technologies can
    enhance 32–4
Piaget, Jean 39, 40, 74
Pittard, V. 10
plug-in 34
podcasting 34, 35
policy initiatives 6–14; first wave 7–9; second
    wave 9–10
politicians: advocates of new technology 7
Postman, Neil 1; *Amusing Ourselves to Death* 4
PowerPoint 5, 54, 88, 98
pragmatists 2, 17
Preston, C. *et al.* 16, 24
Primary National Strategy 58
Priory Woods Special School 68
professional development 117–23; principles
    of 119–20
provisionality: and ICT 67–70

Qualifications and Curriculum Authority 57

reading and writing 4, 65; non-linear
    approach to 65; shared 51–2
Really Simple Syndication (RSS) 35
record-keeping: and assessment 77;
    computer-based 77–9
recording: and ICT 60
reflective mode 4, 5
refuseniks 17
relevance of technology 96
reliability issue: and assessment 76
resistive membranes 47
Reynolds, D. 46
Rogers, Everitt 99
Rogoff, B. 120
Rose, R. 65–6
Ruthven, K. *et al.* 91

St Helens Council 78, *78*
scaffolding 38, 40, 121, 123
'scavenger hunt' 43
Schön, D. 125
school magazines, e-mailed 37
school websites 60, 110–11
science: and ICT 81, 84–5, 121
Scottish Sensory Centre 68
screen-reading software 63
self-assessment 74–5, 77–8
Selinger, M. 120, 121
Selwyn, N. 81, 82, 88
SEN (special educational needs) 55–70; case
    studies 58, 61, 63–4, 66, 68; and choice
    65–6; dissemination of information on
    Internet 57–8; and independence 67–9;
    involvement in own learning 62–3; and
    ipsative assessment 75; key areas essential
    to successful pupil involvement 66;
    reading and writing skills 65; and
    symbol-processing software 64–5; and
    workforce remodelling 60–1; *see also*
    inclusion
shared reading and writing 51–2
Sinclair C5 101–2
Smith, H. *et al.* 48
Social and Emotional Aspects of Learning
    (SEAL) 65
social interaction: and Internet 27–8
social networking 41
software *24*; compatability of 97; flexibility of
    23
Somekh, B. 95
special educational needs *see* SEN
Special Educational Needs and Disabilities
    Act 57
special schools 57
spell-checkers 54
Stevenson Report 7
storyboarding software 54
Strauss, A. and Corbin, J.M. 82
subject pedagogy: and ICT 86–7
subject sub-culture 80, 81–2, 118, 119, 121
subjects/subject areas 80, 81–2; and ICT
    82–6
summative assessment 74
survival stage 99
symbol-processing software 64–5

tablet PCs 48
Taylor, E.W. 123
Teachernet 57

teachers 14, 15–24; benefits of ICT to 16, 23; competence and confidence issue 22, 122; concerns and resistance to ICT 15–16, 23, 95–6, 109; external and internal barriers to using ICT 21–3; imagined conversation between 17–20; and lack of technical support 22; and lack of time 23; and mobile technologies 112–14; and orality 126–7; positive factors needed for successful implementation of ICT 23, *24*; and professional development 117–23; reluctance to use ICT and explanations for 16–17; response types to new technologies 2, 17; rising to the challenge 94–5; and strong pedagogical style 121; and use of ICT in assessment 77
teaching assistants (TAs) 60–1
teaching styles 63–4, 94, 121
technical support 22, *24*, 97
'techno' 1
technological determinism 2–3
technology: harnessing power of 124–9; learning and new 3–5; meaning 1; policy initiatives and new 6–11; progress in 1; and teachers 2, 15–24
technophobia 17, 108–9
technophiles 17
television 2, 4, 99, *100*
texting 128
time, lack of 23
timetable restructuring 23
Tomlinson Review 29
Tools for Schools 105
trackerballs 62
traditionalists 2, 17
Transforming Primacy ICT 17
transition, educational 66
transparent technology 96
triadic assessment 75
Triggs, P.: and John, P.D. 37; and Matthewman, S. 90
Type A/B resource 88

u-learning 113
UltraLab 34
United States: personalised learning 29
upgrades 101

usability issue 99

validity issue: and assessment 76
video-conferencing 34, 45, 95
Virtual Learning Environments (VLEs) 37, 70
virtuous circle 100–1
visual impairment 63, 68
visualisers 51, 52
Vygotsky, L.S. 37, 39, 39–40, 51

Walsh, Ben 16
Watson, D.M. 81, 92
Web 2.0 27
web logs 74
web pages 27, 37
websites, school 60, 110–11
Wenger, E. 82, 90, 125
Westheimer, J. and Kahne, J. 119
Wheeler, S. and Winter, A. 109
whiteboard *see* IWBs
whole-class word/sentence level 52–3, *52*, *53*
wiki spaces 41–2
Wikipedia 41, 42
wikis 128
Williams, P. 9
wireless devices 77; mobile 115
wireless graphics pads 48
wireless keyboards 48
Wokingham Local Education Authority 79, *79*
Woodrow, Derek 45
Woolgar, S. 120
word/sentence level work, whole-class 52–3
workbench communities 120
workforce flexibility 7
workforce remodelling: and ICT 60–1
World Wide Web 41, 128 *see also* Internet
writing: and interactive technologies 54; for real audiences 37; *see also* reading and writing

Yellis 29
Yocum 119
YouTube 128

zone of proximal development (ZPD) 39, 40, 51